Essential

Korean
phrase book

D1120958

Compiled by
**Soyeung Koh
& Gene Baik**

PERIPLUS

Published by Periplus Editions (HK) Ltd.

ISBN: 0-7946-0041-7

Printed in Singapore

Distributed by:

Asia-Pacific
Berkeley Books Pte Ltd
130 Joo Seng Road, 06-01/03
Singapore 368357
Tel: (65) 6280 1330
Fax: (65) 6280 6290
E-mail: inquiries@periplus.com.sg

Japan & Korea
Tuttle Publishing
Yaekari Bldg., 3F
5-4-12 Osaki, Shinagawa-ku
Tokyo 141-0032
Japan
Tel: (03) 5437 0171
Fax: (03) 5437 0755
E-mail: tuttle-sales@gol.com

North America
Tuttle Publishing
Airport Industrial Park
364 Innovation Drive
North Clarendon, VT 05759-9436
USA
Tel: (802) 773 8930
Fax: (802) 773 6993
E-mail: info@tuttlepublishing.com

Indonesia
PT Java Books Indonesia
Jl. Kelapa Gading Kirana
Blok A14 No. 17
Jakarta 14240
Indonesia
Tel: (62-21) 451 5351
Fax: (62-21) 453 4987
E-mail: cs@javabooks.co.id

Contents

Introduction

● **Welcome to the Periplus Essential Phrase Books series, covering the most popular European and Asian languages and containing everything you'd expect from a comprehensive language series. They're concise, accessible and easy to understand, and you'll find them indispensable on your trip abroad.**

Each guide is divided into 15 themed sections and starts with a pronunciation table which explains the phonetic pronunciation to all the words and phrases you'll need to know for your trip, while at the back of the book is an extensive word list and grammar guide which will help you construct basic sentences in your chosen language.

Throughout the book you'll come across colored boxes with a 🖐 beside them. These are designed to help you if you can't understand what your listener is saying to you. Hand the book over to them and encourage them to point to the appropriate answer to the question you are asking.

Other colored boxes in the book - this time without the symbol - give alphabetical listings of themed words with their English translations beside them.

For extra clarity, we have put all English words and phrases in black, foreign language terms in red and their phonetic pronunciation in italic.

This phrase book covers all subjects you are likely to come across during the course of your visit, from reserving a room for the night to ordering food and drink at a restaurant and what to do if your car breaks down or you lose your traveler's checks and money. With over 2,000 commonly used words and essential phrases at your fingertips you can rest assured that you will be able to get by in all situations, so let the Essential Phrase Book become your passport to a secure and enjoyable trip!

Pronunciation guide

Transcriptions

Korean words and expressions in this book are romanized using the
Revised Romanization of Korean prepared and authorized by the Korean
Government (see below). Along with the principles of this system, some
transcription conventions are adopted as follows:

(a) Words are romanized according to sound rather than to Korean
spelling. However, in the case of verbs in the glossary section, the
transcription of tensed sounds has been minimized so that the user
can identify and utilize the verb stem without much confusion (e.g.
to be = *itda*, instead of *itta*).

(b) Where there is an expression consisting of more than one word, a
space is given to mark the word boundary.

(c) Where necessary, a dot (.) is used to mark the syllable boundary so
that confusion in pronunciation can be avoided.

(d) Three dots (...) are used in a grammatical phrase where a noun is
required.

(e) In the glossary index, a hyphen (-) is used to indicate a verb stem or
the optional adjective form derived from an adjectival verb.

(f) In the glossary index, for descriptive words, both adjectival verb
forms (e.g. to be pretty = *yeppeuda*) and adjective forms (e.g. pretty
= *yeppeun*) are given.

The Korean alphabet and its romanization

1) Consonants
   (a) Simple consonants

ㄱ	g, k	ㄴ	n	ㄷ	d, t	ㄹ	r, l	ㅁ m
ㅂ	b, p	ㅅ	s	ㅇ	ng	ㅈ	j	ㅊ ch
ㅋ	k	ㅌ	t	ㅍ	p	ㅎ	h	

   (b) Double consonants

ㄲ	kk	ㄸ	tt	ㅃ	pp	ㅆ	ss	ㅉ jj

2) Vowels
   (a) Simple vowels

ㅏ	a	ㅓ	eo	ㅗ	o	ㅜ	u	─ eu
ㅣ	i	ㅐ	ae	ㅔ	e	ㅚ	oe	ㅟ wi

   (b) Compound vowels

ㅑ	ya	ㅕ	yeo	ㅛ	yo	ㅠ	yu	ㅒ yae
ㅖ	ye	ㅘ	wa	ㅙ	wae	ㅝ	wo	ㅞ we
ㅢ	ui							

Reading romanized Korean

There is a very important distinction between the reading of romanized
Korean and English. The Korean romanization system depicts the sound
of Korean in English letters to help foreigners communicate in Korean.
Because English letters used in romanized Korean are sound symbols,

they have to be pronounced in a certain way only. They should not be treated as those in English words. In English words, the sound value assigned to a certain letter varies according to different words. For example, 'a' in *apple, father, syllable* and *date* all have different sound values. Unless you have learnt the English phonetic symbols, you might read romanized Korean 'a' differently from the expected sound depending on what romanized Korean words you have. For example, you might read a as 'a' in *apple* when you get the romanized Korean word *sam* (삼) 'three'; or you might read it as 'a' in *syllable* for either *a* in the romanized Korean word *saram* (사람) 'person', etc.

To avoid this type of confusion, some examples of English words containing sounds equivalent to some of the romanized Korean vowels and consonants are given as follow (approximate guideline only):

Vowels: *eo, eu, ae* and *oe* are single vowels in romanized Korean as shown below. Therefore careful attention should be given to these vowels in not splitting them into two. Also, careful attention should be given to *u* [우] not to be read as English 'you'. Some common vowels which might confuse you are:

a	아	**ah**, f**a**ther	(but shorter)
eo	어	b**ir**d, s**er**ve	
o	오	b**a**ll, p**o**re	(but shorter)
u	우	sh**oe**, sch**oo**l	(but shorter)
eu	으	br**o**ken, g**o**lden	
i	이	b**ee**, sh**ee**p	(but shorter)
ae	애	**a**pple, b**a**d	
e	에	b**e**d, **e**gg	
oe	외	w**e**t, w**e**lcome	

Consonants: There won't be much trouble in pronouncing romanized Korean consonants except some tensed ones which require a relatively strong muscular effort in the vocal organs without the expulsion of air. Some examples are given as follow:

kk	ㄲ	s**k**i, s**k**y	(k after s)
tt	ㄸ	s**t**eak, s**t**ing	(t after s)
pp	ㅃ	s**p**eak, s**p**y	(p after s)
ss	ㅆ	**s**ea, **s**ir	(s before a vowel)
jj	ㅉ	bri**dg**e, mi**dg**et	(similar to a tutting sound in an exhaling way)

1

Useful lists

Useful lists

1 .1 **T**oday or tomorrow?

What day is it today?	오늘은 무슨 요일이에요?	*oneureun museun yoirieyo?*
Today's Monday	오늘은 월요일이에요	*oneureun woryoir-ieyo*
- Tuesday	화요일이에요	*hwayoir-ieyo*
- Wednesday	수요일이에요	*suyoir-ieyo*
- Thursday	목요일이에요	*mogyoir-ieyo*
- Friday	금요일이에요	*geumyoir-ieyo*
- Saturday	토요일이에요	*toyoir-ieyo*
- Sunday	일요일이에요	*iryoir-ieyo*
in January	일월에	*irwore*
since February	이월부터	*iwobuteo*
in spring	봄에	*bome*
in summer	여름에	*yeoreume*
in autumn	가을에	*gaeure*
in winter	겨울에	*gyeoure*
2001	이천 일년	*icheon illyeon*
the twentieth century	이십 세기	*isip segi*
the twenty-first century	이십일 세기	*isibil segi*
What's the date today?	오늘이 몇 일이에요?	*oneuri myeochirieyo?*
Today's the 24th	오늘은 이십 사일이에요	*oneureun isip sairieyo*
Monday 3 November	십일월 삼일, 월요일이에요	*sibirwol samil, woryoirieyo*
in the morning	아침에	*achime*
in the afternoon	오후에	*ohue*
in the evening	저녁에	*jeonyeoge*
at night	밤에	*bame*
this morning	오늘 아침	*oneul achim*

9

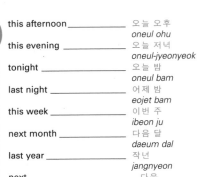

this afternoon	오늘 오후	*oneul ohu*
this evening	오늘 저녁	*oneul-jyeonyeok*
tonight	오늘 밤	*oneul bam*
last night	어제 밤	*eojet bam*
this week	이번 주	*ibeon ju*
next month	다음 달	*daeum dal*
last year	작년	*jangnyeon*
next...	... 다음	*...da-eum*
in...days/weeks/months/ years	... 일 / 주 / 달 / 년 후에	*...il/ju/dal/nyeon hue*
...weeks ago	... 주 전	
day off	비번, 쉬는 날	*bibeon, swineunnal*

🔴 .2 Legal holidays

● **National holidays** in Korea are:

January 1: New Year's Day	설날	*Seolnal*
January: Korean New Year's Day (Lunar)	설날	*Seolnal*
March 1: Samil Independence Movement Day	삼일절	*Samiljeol*

This celebrates the independence movement in 1919 against Japanese colonial rule.

April 5: Arbor Day	식목일	*Singmogil*

This is a day designated for planting trees at nearby mountains and parks.

April: Buddha's Birthday (Lunar)	석가탄신일	*Seokkatansinil*

This day celebrates the birth of Buddha; on the eve, a street parade with multi-colored lanterns is held.

May 5: Children's Day	어린이날	*Eorininal*
June 6: Memorial Day	현충일	*Hyeonchung-il*

This day pays tribute to those who sacrificed their lives for the country.

July 17: Constitution Day	제헌절	*Jeheonjeol*
August 15: Liberation Day	광복절	*Gwangbokjeol*

This day celebrates Korea's liberation from Japanese colonization, which lasted 36 years.

August: Thanksgiving Day (Lunar)	추석	*Chuseok*

Chuseok is the most important traditional holiday; everyone heads for their hometown, so heavy traffic congestion on major highways should be expected for all three days.

October 3: National Foundation Day	개천절	*Gaecheonjeol*
December 25: Christmas Day	성탄절	*Seongtanjeol*

.3 What time is it?

What time is it? _____	지금 몇 시예요?	jigeum myeot-siyeyo?
It's nine o'clock _____	아홉시예요	ahopsieyo
- five past ten _____	열 시 오 분이에요	yeolsi obunieyo
- a quarter past eleven_____	열 한시 십오분이에요	yeolhansi sibobunieyo
- twenty past twelve _____	열 두시 이십 분 이에요	yeol dusi isipbun ieyo
- half past one _____	한시 반 이에요	hansi banieyo
- twenty-five to three _____	세시 이십오분 전이에요	sesi isibobun jeonieyo
- a quarter to four _____	네시 십오분 전이에요	nesi sibobun jeonieyo
- ten to five _____	다섯시 십분 전이에요	daseotsi sipbun jeonieyo
It's midday (twelve noon) __	정오(낮 열 두시)예요	jeong-o(nat yeoldusi)-eyo
It's midnight _____	자정(밤 열 두시)이에요	jajeong(bam yeoldusi)-ieyo
half an hour _____	삼십 분	samsipbun
What time? _____	몇 시예요?	myeot siyeyo?
What time can I come _____ by?	몇 시에 가면 돼요?	myeot sie gamyeon dwaeyo?
At... _____	... 에	...e
After... _____	... 후에	... hue
Before... _____	... 전에	...jeone
Between...and...(o'clock) ___	...시 에서... 시 사이에	...sieseo...si saie
From...to... _____	...부터... 까지	...buteo...kkaji
In...minutes _____	... 분 후에	...bun hue
- an hour _____	한 시간 후에	hansigan hue
-...hours _____	...시간 후에	...sigan hue
- a quarter of an hour_____	십 오분 후에	sibobun hue
- three quarters of an hour _	사십 오분 후에	sasibobun hue
too early/late_____	너무 일찍/ 늦게	neomu iljjik/ neutge
on time_____	정 각에	jeonggage
summertime (daylight _____ saving)	써머 타임	sseomeo taim

Useful lists

0	영
	yeong
1	일
	il
2	이
	i
3	삼
	sam
4	사
	sa
5	오
	o
6	육
	yuk
7	칠
	chil
8	팔
	pal
9	구
	gu
10	십
	sip
11	십일
	sibil
12	십이
	sibi
13	십삼
	sipsam
14	십사
	sipsa
15	십오
	sibo
16	십육
	simnyuk
17	십칠
	sipchil
18	십팔
	sip-pal
19	십구
	sip-gu
20	이십
	isip
21	이십일
	isibil
22	이십이
	isibi
30	삼십
	samsip
31	삼십일
	samsibil
32	삼십이
	samsibi
40	사십
	sasip

50	오십 *osip*
60	육십 *yuksip*
70	칠십 *chilsip*
80	팔십 *palsip*
90	구십 *gusip*
100	백 *baek*
101	백일 *baegil*
110	백십 *baek sip*
120	백이십 *baegisip*
200	이백 *ibaek*
300	삼백 *sambaek*
400	사백 *sabaek*
500	오백 *obaek*
600	육백 *yukbaek*
700	칠백 *chilbaek*
800	팔백 *palbaek*
900	구백 *gubaek*
1,000	천 *cheon*
1,100	천백 *cheon baek*
2,000	이천 *icheon*
10,000	만 *man*
100,000	십만 *simman*
1,000,000	백만 *baeng-man*
1st	첫 번째/ 첫째 *cheot beonjjae/cheotjjae*
2nd	두 번째/ 둘째 *du beonjjae/duljjae*
3rd	세 번째/ 셋째 *se beonjjae/setjjae*
4th	네 번째/ 넷째 *ne beonjjae/netjjae*
5th	다섯 번째/ 다섯째 *daseot beonjjae/daseotjjae*

6th	여섯 번째/ 여섯째	*yeoseot beonjjae/yeoseotjjae*
7th	일곱 번째/ 일곱째	*ilgop beonjjae/ilgopjjae*
8th	여덟 번째/ 여덟째	*yeodeol beonjjae/yeodeoljjae*
9th	아홉 번째/ 아홉째	*ahop beonjjae/ahopjjae*
10th	열 번째/열째	*yeol beonjjae/yeoljjae*
11th	열 한번째	*yeol hanbeonjjae*
12th	열 두번째	*yeol dubeonjjae*
13th	열 세번째	*yeol sebeonjjae*
14th	열 네번째	*yeol nebeonjjae*
15th	열 다섯번째	*yeol daseotbeonjjae*
16th	열 여섯번째	*yeol yeoseotbeonjjae*
17th	열 일곱번째	*yeol ilgopbeonjjae*
18th	열 여덟번째	*yeol yeodeolbeonjjae*
19th	열 아홉번째	*yeol ahopbeonjjae*
20th	스무 번째	*seumubeonjjae*
21st	스물 한 번째	*seumul hanbeonjjae*
22nd	스물 두 번째	*seumul dubeonjjae*
30th	서른 번째	*seoreunbeonjjae*
100th	백 번째	*baekbeonjjae*
1,000th	천 번째	*cheonbeonjjae*
once	한 번	*hanbeon*
twice	두 번	*dubeon*
double	두 배	*dubae*
triple	세 배	*sebae*
half	반	*ban*
a quarter	사분의 일	*sabunui il*
a third	삼분의 일	*sambunui il*

some/a few	조금
	jogeum
2 + 4 = 6	이 더하기 사 는 육
	i deohagi saneun yuk
4 - 2 = 2	사 빼기 이 는 이
	sa bbaegi ineun i
2 x 4 = 8	이 곱하기 사 는 팔
	i gopagi saneun pal
4 ÷ 2 = 2	사 나누기 이 는 이
	sa nanugi ineun i
even/odd	짝수/ 홀수
	jjaksu/holsu
total	합(계)
	hap(gye)
6 x 9	육 곱하기 구
	yuk gopagi gu

.5 The weather

Is the weather going to be good/bad?	날 씨가 좋을 /나쁠까요?
	nalssiga joe-ul/nappeulkkayo?
Is it going to get colder/hotter?	날 씨가 추울 / 더울까요?
	nalssiga chuul/deo-ulkkayo?
What temperature is it going to be?	기온이 얼마나 될까요?
	gioni eolmana doelkkayo?
Is it going to rain?	비가 올까요?
	biga olkkayo?
Is there going to be a storm?	폭풍이 올까요?
	pokpung-i olkkayo?
Is it going to snow?	눈이 올까요?
	nuni olkkayo?
Is it going to freeze?	길이 얼 올까요?
	gili eoleulkkayo?
Is the thaw setting in?	녹기 시작해요?
	nokgi sijakheyo?
Is it going to be foggy?	안개가 낄까요?
	angaega kkilkkayo?
Is there going to be a thunderstorm?	천둥이 칠까요?
	cheondungi chilkkayo?
The weather's changing	날 씨가 바뀌고 있어요
	nalssiga bakkwigo itseoyo
It's going to be cold	날이 추워질 거예요
	nari chuweojil geoyeoyo
What's the weather going to be like today/ tomorrow?	오늘/내일 날씨는 어떨까요?
	oneul/nae-il nalssineun eotteolkkayo?

무더운	화창한	맑은
sweltering/muggy	**sunny**	**fine**
서리	밤 서리	얼음/ 길이 언
frost	**overnight frost**	**ice/icy**
비	강풍	폭우/ 호우
rain	**gusts of wind**	**downpour**

쌀쌀한	우박	서늘한/ 시원한
frost/frosty	hail	cool
쾌청한 날	숨막히게 더운	눈
sunny day	stifling	snow
맑은/ 구름 낀/ 잔뜩	적당한/강한/매우 강	허리케인/ 태풍
흐린 하늘	한 바람	hurricane
clear skies/cloudy/	moderate/strong/	으스스한
overcast	very strong winds	bleak
매우 더운	온화한	구름이 낀/ 흐린
very hot	mild	cloudiness
...도 (영하/ 영상)	폭풍	바람
...degrees (below/	storm	wind
above zero)	춥고 습한	바람 부는
맑은	cold and damp	windy
fine/clear	안개/ 안개가 자욱한	혹서
폭우	fog/foggy	heatwave
heavy rain	눅눅한/ 습한	
	humid	

.6 Here, there...

See also 5.1 Asking for directions

here, over here / there, _____ 여기/ 저기
  over there
  yeogi/jeogi
somewhere/nowhere _____ 어딘가에/ 아무데도
  eodin-gae/amudedo
everywhere _____ 어디에나
  eodiena
far away/nearby _____ 멀리/ 가까이에 (근처에)
  meolli/gakkaie(geuncheoe)
(on the) right/(on the) left _ 오른 쪽/ 왼 쪽
  oreun jjok/oen jjok
to the right/left of _____ 오른 쪽으로/ 왼 쪽으로
  oreun jjogro/oen jjogro
straight ahead _____ 바로 앞
  baro ap
via _____ ...를 지나
  ...reul jina
in _____ ...안에
  ...ane
to _____ ...로
  ...ro
on _____ ...위에
  ...wie
under _____ ...아래
  ...arae
opposite/facing _____ 맞은 편에
  majeunpyeone
next to _____ ...옆에
  ...yeope
near _____ ...근처에
  ...geuncheo-e

in front of	...앞에 ...ape
in the center	가운데에 gaundee
forward	앞으로 apro
down	아래로 araero
up	위로 wiro
inside	안의/안에 anui/ane
outside	바깥쪽의(에) bakkatjjogui/bakkatjjoge
behind	뒤에 dwie
at the front	앞에 ape
at the back	뒤에 dwie
in the north	북쪽에 bukjjoge
to the south	남쪽으로 namjjogeuro
from the west	서쪽에서 seojjogeseo
from the east	동쪽에서 dongjjogeseo
to the...of	의...쪽으로 ui ...jjogeuro

.7 What does that sign say?

See 5.4 Traffic signs

대여 **for hire**	식수 **drinking water**	호텔 **hotel**
매진 **sold out**	사용 금지 **not in use**	고장 **out of order**
대기실 **waiting room**	미시오 **push**	관광 안내소 **tourist information bureau**
온수/냉수 **hot/cold water**	세 놓음 **for rent**	정지 **stop**
비상 제동장치 **emergency brake**	화장실 **bathrooms**	매물 **for sale**
화재시 탈출구/ 에스칼레이터 **fire escape/escalator**	당기시오 **pull**	우체국 **post office**

17

고압	사용 중	(시립) 경찰
high voltage	**engaged**	**(municipal) police**
안내	금연/쓰레기 투기 금	현금 출납원
information	지	**cashier**
비상구	**no smoking/no litter**	위험/화재 위험
emergency exit	매표소	**danger/fire hazard**
영업 중	**ticket office**	입구
open	운행표	**entrance**
입장 (무료)	**timetable**	문 닫음
admission (free)	접근 금지/출입금지	**closed**
매물	**no access/no entry**	교통 순경
for sale	경찰	**traffic police**
개 조심	**police**	사냥/낚시 금지
beware of the dog	병원	**no hunting/fishing**
손 대지 마시오	**hospital**	만원
please do not	소방서	*full*
disturb/touch	**fire department**	응급 처치
페인트 주의	환전	**first aid/accident and**
wet paint	**exchange**	**emergency (hospital)**
위험	보행자	예약석
danger	**pedestrians**	**reserved**

1.8 Personal details

surname_____	성
	seong
first name _____	이름
	ireum
initials_____	이닛샬
	initsyal
address (street/number) ___	주소 (가 /번지)
	juso (ga/beonji)
postal code/town_____	우편번호/ 시
	upyeon-beonho/ si
sex (male/female) _____	성 (남성/ 여성)
	seong (namseong/yeoseong)
nationality _____	국적
	gukjeok
date of birth _____	생년월일
	saengnyeonworil
place of birth _____	출생지
	chulsaengji
occupation_____	직업
	jigeop
marital status _____	결혼 여부
	gyeolhon-yeobu
married/single _____	기혼/ 미혼
	gihon/mihon
widowed _____	사별한
	sabyeolhan
(number of) children _____	자녀(수)
	janyeo(su)

passport/identity card/driving license number
여권/ 신분증/ 운전면허 번호
yeokkwon/sinbunjjeung/unjeonmyeonheo beonho

place and date of issue
발행 기관 및 일자
balhaeng gigwan mit iljja

signature
서명
seo.myeong

Useful lists

2

Courtesies

Courtesies

● **Koreans** greet each other with a little bow. Younger people are expected to make a deep bow to show their respect to the elderly. Handshakes are exchanged among adults, but it is not very acceptable when greeting a woman.

.1 **G**reetings

Good morning/ afternoon/evening	안녕하세요 *annyeonghaseyo*
Hello Peter, how are things?	안녕하세요 피터씨 일은 잘 되세요? *annyeonghaseyo piteossi ireun jal doeseyo?*
Hi Helen; fine, thank you, and you?	네 헬렌씨 안녕하세요? *ne helenssi annyeonghaseyo?*
Very well, and you?	네 어떻게 지내세요? *ne eoddeokke jinaeseyo?*
In excellent health/ In great shape	네 잘지내요 *ne jaljinaeyo*
So-so	그저 그래요 *geujeo geuraeyo*
Not very well	아주 좋지는 않네요 *aju jochineun anneyo*
Not bad	그냥 지내요 *geunyang jinaeyo*
I'm going to leave	가봐야 겠어요 *gabwaya gesseoyo*
I have to be going, someone's waiting for me	지금 누가 기다리고 있어서 가야겠어요 *jigeum nuga gidarigo isseoseo gayagesseoyo*
Good-bye	안녕히 가세요 *annyeonghi gaseyo*
See you later	또 봐요 *tto bwayo*
See you soon	다시 봐요 *dasi bwayo*
See you in a little while	조만간 다시 봐요. *jomangan dasi bwayo.*
Sweet dreams	잘 자요 *jal jayo*
Good night	안녕히 주무세요 *annyeonghi jumuseyo*
All the best/Have fun	잘 지내세요 *jal jinaeseyo*
Good luck	행운을 빌어요 *haeng-uneul bireoyo*
Have a nice vacation	휴가 잘 보내세요 *huga jal bonaeseyo*
Bon voyage/Have a good trip	여행 잘 다녀 오세요 *yeohaeng jal danyeo oseyo*
Thank you, the same to you	고마워요, 잘 지내세요 *gomawoyo, jal jinaeseyo*
Say hello to/Give my regards to...	... 에게 안부 전해 주세요 *...ege anbu jeonhae juseyo*

.2 How to ask a question

Who?	누구? *nugu?*
Who's that?/Who is it?/Who's there?	누구세요? *nuguseyo?*
What?	뭐예요? *mwoyeoyo?*
What is there to see?	볼 것이 있나요? *Bol gesi innayo?*
What category of hotel is it?	무슨 급 호텔이에요? *museun geup hotelieyo?*
Where?	어디에요? *eodieyo?*
Where's the bathroom?	화장실이 어디에요? *hwajangsiri eodieyo?*
Where are you going?	어디 가세요? *eodi gaseyo?*
Where are you from?	어디서 왔어요? *eodiseo wasseoyo?*
How far is that?	얼마나 멀어요? *eolmana meoreoyo?*
How long does that take?	얼마나 걸려요? *eolmana geollyeoyo?*
How long is the trip?	여행은 얼마나 걸리나요? *yeohaengeun eolmana geollinayo?*
How much?	얼마예요? *eolmayeyo?*
How much is this?	이거 얼마예요? *igeo eolmayeyo?*
What time is it?	몇 시예요? *myeot siyeyo?*
Which one/s?	어느 것? *eoneu geot?*
Which glass is mine?	어느 컵이 내거예요? *eoneu keobi naekkeoyeyo?*
When?	언제요? *eonjeyo?*
When are you leaving?	언제 떠나요? *eonje ddeonayo?*
Why?	왜요? *waeyo?*
Why are you leaving?	왜 가세요? *wae gaseyo?*
Could you...?	알려주세요 *...ayeo juseyo?*
Could you help me/ give me a hand please?	(좀) 도와주세요 *(jom) dowajuseyo*
Could you point that out to me/show me please?	어떻게 가는지 가르쳐 주세요 *eotteoke ganeunji gareuchyeo juseyo*
Could you come with me, please?	같이 좀 가 주세요 *gachi jom gajuseyo*
Could you reserve/ book me some tickets please?	예약 좀 해 주세요 *yeyak jom hae juseyo*
Could you recommend another hotel?	다른 호텔을 좀 알려주세요 *dareun hotereul jom allyeojuseyo*

Do you know...? _____	... 아세요?
	...aseyo?
Do you know _____ whether...?	... 인지 아세요?
	...inji aseyo?
Do you have...? _____	... 있어요?
	... isseoyo?
Do you have a ... for _____ me?	...있으세요?
	isseuseyo?
Do you have a vegetarian ___ dish, please?	채식 되나요?
	chaesik doeanyo?
I would like... _____	... 주세요
	...juseyo
I'd like a kilo of _____ apples, please	사과 일 킬로 주세요
	sagwa il killo juseyo
Can/May I? _____	... 돼요?
	...dwaeyo?
Can/May I take this _____ away?	이거 가져가도 돼요?
	igeo gajyeogado dwaeyo?
Can I smoke here? _____	여기서 담배 피워도 돼요?
	yeogiseo dambae piwodo dwaeyo?
Could I ask you _____ something?	뭐 좀 물어봐도 돼요?
	mwo jom mureobwado dwaeyo?

2 .3 How to reply

Yes, of course _____	네, 물론이죠
	ne, mullonijyo
No, I'm sorry _____	죄송하지만 안 돼요
	joesong-hajiman andwaeyo
Yes, what can I do _____ for you?	네 뭘 도와드릴까요?
	ne, mwol dowadrilkkayo?
Just a moment, _____ please	잠시만요
	jamsimanyo
No, I don't have _____ time now	아니오, 지금 시간이 없어요
	aniyo, jigeum sigani eobseoyo
No, that's impossible _____	아니오, 안돼요
	aniyo, andwaeyo
I think so/I think that's _____ absolutely right	네, 맞아요
	ne, majayo
I think so too/I agree _____	저도 그렇게 생각해요
	jeodo geureoke saenggakaeyo
I agree/don't agree _____	네 그래요/그렇지 않아요
	ne geuraeyo/geureochi anayo
OK/it's fine _____	네, 좋아요
	ne, joayo
OK, all right _____	네, 됐어요
	ne, dwaetseoyo
I hope so too _____	그랬으면 좋겠어요
	geuraesseumyeon jokesseoyo
No, not at all/ _____ Absolutely not	전혀 아니에요/ 절대로 아니에요
	jeonhyeo anieyo/jeoldaero anieyo
No, no one _____	아니오, 아무도요
	aniyo, amudoyo
No, nothing _____	아니오, 아무것도 아니에요
	aniyo, amugeotdo anieyo
That's right _____	맞아요
	majayo

Something's wrong _____ 뭐가 잘 못 됐어요
mwoga jalmot dwaesseoyo
Perhaps/maybe _____ 아마도요
amadoyo
I don't know _____ 잘 모르겠어요
jal moreugesseoyo

2 .4 Thank you

Thank you _____ 고마워요
gomawoyo
Thank you for... _____ ...해줘서 고마워요
...haejwoseo gomawoyo
Thank you very much _____ 감사합니다
gamsahammida
You shouldn't have _____ 이렇게까지 해주셔서 감사합니다
ireokekkaji hae jusyeoseo gamsahammida
I enjoyed it very much _____ 즐거웠어요
jeulgeowosseoyo
You're welcome _____ 괜찮아요 / 아니에요
gwaenchanayo/anieyo
My pleasure/don't _____ 별 말씀을요
mention it *beol malsseumeulyo*
That's all right _____ 괜찮아요
gwaenchanayo
Excuse me (starting to _____ 실례합니다
speak to a stranger) *sillye hammida*

2 .5 Sorry

Excuse me/pardon _____ 뭐라고 하셨어요?
(asking to repeat *mworago hasyeosseoyo?*
what's been said)
I'm sorry _____ 죄송해요
joesonghaeyo
I do apologize _____ 사과 드려요
sagwa deuryeoyo
Sorry, I didn't know _____ 죄송해요, ...몰랐어요
that... *joesonghaeyo,...mollasseoyo*
I didn't mean it/It was _____ 일부러 그런 건 아니에요
an accident *ilbureo geureongeon anieyo*
That's all right/Don't _____ 괜찮아요/ 걱정 마세요
worry about it *gwaenchanayo/geokjeong maseyo*
Never mind/Forget it _____ 아무 일도 아니에요
amuildo anieyo
It could happen to _____ 그럴 수도 있죠
anyone *geureol sudo itjyo*

2 .6 What do you think?

Which do you prefer/ _____ 어떤 게 더 좋아요?
like best? *eotteonge deo joayo?*
What do you think? _____ 어떻게 생각해요?
eotteoke saenggakhaeyo?
Don't you like dancing? _____ 춤 추는 거 좋아하지 않으세요?
chumchuneun geo joahaji aneuseyo?

I don't mind _____	상관없어요
	sang-gwan eobseoyo
Great/Wonderful _____	훌륭해요/ 좋아요
	hullyunghaeyo/joayo
I'm very happy/ _____ delighted to...	...해서 좋아요
	...haeseo joayo
I'm glad that... _____	...해서 좋아요
	...haeseo joayo
It's really nice here _____	여기 참 좋네요
	yeogi cham jonneyo
How nice for you! _____	참 잘 됐군요
	cham jal dwaessgunyo
I'm (not) very happy_____ with...	...가 좋아요/싫어요
	...ga joayo/sireoyo
I'm having a great time ____	재미있어요
	jaemiisseoyo
I can't wait till tomorrow/ __ I'm looking forward to tomorrow	빨리 내일이 왔으면 좋겠어요
	ppalli naeiri wasseumyeon jokesseoyo
I hope it works out _____	잘 됐으면 좋겠어요
	jal dwaesseumyeon jokesseoyo
How awful!/What a _____ pity!/What a shame!	저런
	jeoreon
What nonsense/_____ How silly/ That's ridiculous!	말도 안돼요
	maldo andwaeyo
How disgusting! _____	정말 끔찍해요
	jeongmal kkeumjikaeyo
I don't like it/them _____	마음에 안 들어요
	maeume andeureyo
I'm fed up/bored _____	지겨워요
	jigyeowoyo
This is no good _____	이건 안 돼요
	igeon andwaeyo
This is not what I_____ expected	이건 아니지요
	igeon anijiyo

Conversation

3

Conversation

3.1 I beg your pardon?

I don't speak any/_____ I speak a little...	...말은 전혀/조금밖에 못해요 ...mareun jeonhyeo/ jogeumbakke moteyo
I'm American _____	저는 미국 사람이에요 jeoneun miguksaramieyo
Do you speak English?_____	영어 할 줄 아세요? yeong-eo haljjul aseyo?
Is there anyone who_____ speaks...?	...말 할 줄 아는 사람 있어요? ...mal haljjul aneun saram isseoyo?
I beg your pardon/What?___	뭐라고 했어요? mworago haesseoyo?
I don't understand_____	잘 모르겠어요 jal moreugesseoyo
Do you understand me? ___	알겠어요? algesseoyo?
Could you repeat that, _____ please?	다시 말씀해 주세요 dasi malsseumhae juseyo
Could you speak more_____ slowly, please?	천천히 말씀해 주세요 cheoncheonhi malsseumhae juseyo
What does that mean?_____	그게 무슨 뜻이에요? geuge museun tteusieyo?
What does that word _____ mean?	그 단어가 무슨 뜻이에요? geu daneoga museun tteusieyo?
It's more or less the _____ same as...	...와 비슷해요 ...wa biseuthaeyo
Could you write that_____ down for me, please?	그걸 적어 주시겠어요 geugeol jeogeo jusigesseoyo
Could you spell that _____ for me, please?	철자로 말해 주세요 cheoljarol malhae juseyo
Could you point that_____ out in this phrase book, please?	이 책 어디에 적혀 있는지 가르쳐 주세요 i chaek eodie jeokyeo inneunji gareuchyeo juseyo
Just a minute, I'll look _____ it up	잠깐만요, 찾아 볼게요 jamkkanmanyo, chajabolkkeyo
I can't find the word/the ___ sentence	그 단어를/ 문장을 찾을 수 없어요 geu daneoreul/munjang-eul chajeul su eopseoyo
How do you say that in...? _	...말로 그건 어떻게 말하나요? ...mallo geugeon eoddeokke malhanayo?
How do you pronounce_____ that?	어떻게 발음하나요? eotteoke bareumhanayo?

3.2 Introductions

May I introduce myself? ___	제 소개를 할게요 je sogereul halkkeyo
My name's... _____	제 이름은...입니다 je ireumeun...immida
I'm... _____	저는...입니다 jeoneun...immida
What's your name?_____	이름이 뭐에요? ireumi mwoeyo?

Conversation

May I introduce...?	...를 소개할게요	
	...reul sogehalkkeyo	
This is my wife/husband	제 처 /남편이에요	
	je cheo /nampyeon-ieyo	
This is my daughter/son	제 딸/아들입니다	
	je ttar/adeur-immida	
This is my mother/father	제 어머니/아버지이십니다	
	je eomeoni/abeoji-simmida	
This is my fiancée/fiancé	제 약혼녀/약혼자에요	
	je yakonnyeo/yakonja-eyo	
This is my friend	제 친구에요	
	je chin-gueyo	
How do you do?	만나서 반가워요	
	manaseo ban-gawoyo	
Hi, pleased to meet you	안녕하세요, 만나서 반가워요.	
	Annyeonghaseyo, manaseo ban-gawoyo	
Pleased to meet you	만나서 반갑습니다	
	manaseo ban-gapseummida	
Where are you from?	어디서 왔어요?	
	eodiseo wasseoyo?	
I'm American	미국에서요	
	migugeseoyo.	
What city do you live in?	어느 도시에 살아요?	
	eoneu dosie sarayo?	
In...near...	... 근처... 에 살아요	
	...geuncheo ...e sarayo	
Have you been here long?	여기 오래 있었어요?	
	yeogi orae isseosseoyo?	
A few days	며칠 있었어요	
	myeochil isseosseoyo	
How long are you staying here?	여기 얼마나 오래 계실 거에요?	
	yeogi eolmana orae gyesil geoeyo?	
We're (probably) leaving tomorrow/in two weeks	(아마) 내일/ 이 주 후에 떠날 거에요	
	(ama) naeil/ijuhue tteonalgeoeyo	
Where are you staying?	어디에 계세요?	
	eodie gyeseyo?	
I'm staying in a hotel/an apartment	호텔에/ 아파트에 있어요	
	hotere/apateue isseoyo	
At a campsite	야영장에	
	yayeongjange	
I'm staying with friends/relatives	친구들/ 친척들하고 같이 있어요	
	chin-gudeul/chincheokdeul hago gachi isseoyo.	
Are you here on your own?	여기에 혼자 있어요?	
	yeogie honja isseoyo?	
Are you here with your family?	가족과 함께 있어요?	
	gajokgwa hamkke isseoyo?	
I'm on my own	혼자 있어요	
	honja isseoyo	
I'm with my wife/husband	처/남편과 같이 있어요	
	cheo/nampyeon-gwa gachi isseoyo	
- with my family	- 가족과 같이 있어요	
	gajokkwa gachi isseoyo	
- with relatives	- 친척하고 있어요	
	chincheokhago isseoyo	
- with a friend/friends	- 친구(들)와 같이 있어요	
	chin-gu(deul)wa gachi isseoyo	

Are you married?	결혼 했어요?	gyeolhon haesseoyo?
Are you engaged?	약혼 했어요?	yakhon haesseoyo?
That's none of your business	상관 마세요	sang-gwan maseyo
I'm married	결혼 했어요	gyeolhon haesseoyo
I'm single	미혼 이에요	mihonieyo
I'm not married	결혼 안 했어요	gyeolhon an haesseoyo
I'm separated	별거 중이에요	byeolgeo jungieyo.
I'm divorced	이혼했어요	ihonhaesseoyo.
I'm a widow/widower	혼자됐어요	honja dwaesseoyo
Do you have any children/grandchildren?	자녀는 어떻게 되세요/손자 는 있나요?	janyeoneun eotteoke doeseyo/sonjaneun innayo?
How old are you?	몇 살이에요?	myeotsarieyo?
How old is she/he?	그 사람은 몇 살이에요?	geu sarameun myeotsarieyo?
I'm...(years old)	... 살 이에요	...sarieyo
She's/he's...(years old)	그 사람은...살 이에요	geu sarameun...sarieyo
What do you do for a living?	무슨 일 하세요?	museunil haseyo?
I work in an office	사무실에서 일해요	samusireseo ilhaeyo
I'm a student	학생이에요	haksaengieyo
I'm unemployed	일 안 해요	il anhaeyo
I'm retired	은퇴했어요	euntoe haesseoyo
I'm on a disability pension	장애인 연금 받아요	jang-aein yeongeum badayo
I'm a housewife	가정 주부에요	gajeong jubueyo
Do you like your job?	직장일이 마음에 들어요?	jikjang-ili maeume deureoyo?
Most of the time	대부분은요	daebubuneunyo
Mostly I do, but I prefer vacations	일도 좋아하지만, 휴가가 더 좋아요.	ildo joahajiman, hugaga deo joayo

3.3 Starting/ending a conversation

Could I ask you something?	뭐 좀 물어봐도 돼요?	mwo jom mureobwado dwaeyo?
Excuse me	실례합니다	sillyehammida

Could you help me _____ please?	좀 도와주시겠어요?
	jom dowajusigesseoyo?
Yes, what's the problem? __	네, 무슨 일이세요?
	Ne, museuniriseyo?
What can I do for you? ____	뭘 도와줄까요?
	mwol dowajulgayo?
Sorry, I don't have time____ now	죄송해요, 지금 시간이 없어요.
	joesonghaeyo, jigeum sigani eopseoyo
Do you have a light? _____	불 좀 빌릴 수 있을까요?
	bul jom billilsu isseulkkayo?
May I join you? _____	같이 해도 돼요?
	gachi haedo dwaeyo?
Could you take a picture ___ of me/us?	사진 좀 찍어 줄래요?
	sajin jom jjigeo jullaeyo?
Leave me alone _____	혼자 있게 해주세요
	honja issge haejuseyo
Go away or I'll scream_____	저리 가세요 안 그러면 소리지를 거에요
	jeori gaseyo angeureomyeon sorijireul geoeyo

.4 Congratulations and condolences

Happy birthday	생일 축하합니다
	saeng.il chukahamnida
Please accept my condolences	애도를 표합니다
	aedoreul pyohammida
My deepest sympathy _____	가슴 깊이 애도합니다
	gaseum gipi aedohammida

.5 A chat about the weather

See also 1.5 The weather

It's so hot/cold today!_____	오늘 참 더워요/추워요
	oneul cham deowoyo/chuwoyo
Isn't it a lovely day? _____	날씨 참 좋지 않아요?
	nalssi cham jochi anayo?
It's so windy/what a storm!	바람이 정말 많이 부네요
	barami jeongmal mani buneyo
All that rain/snow! _____	대단한 비/눈야
	dawdanhan bi/nuniya
It's so foggy! _____	안개가 자욱해요
	angaega jaukaeyo
Has the weather been like this for long?	날씨가 오랫동안 이랬나요?
	nalssiga oraetdong.an iraennayo?
Is it always this hot/cold ___ here?	여긴 항상 이렇게 더운가요? /추운가요?
	yeogin hangsang ireoke deoun.gayo/ chuun.gayo?
Is it always this dry/humid _ here?	여긴 항상 이렇게 건조한가요/습한가요?
	yeogin hangsang ireoke geonjohan. gayo/ seuphan.gayo?

.6 Hobbies

Do you have any hobbies? _	무슨 취미가 있으세요?
	museun chwimiga isseuseyo?
I like knitting/reading/_____ photography	뜨개질/ 책 읽기/ 사진찍기를 좋아해요
	tteugaejil/chaegilkki/sajinjjikgi-reul joahaeyo
I enjoy listening to music __	음악 듣는 걸 좋아해요
	eumak deunneun geol joahaeyo
I play the guitar/the piano__	기타를/피아노를 쳐요
	gitareul/pianoreul cheoyo
I like the cinema_____	영화를 좋아해요
	yeonghwareul joahaeyo
I like traveling/playing _____ sports/going fishing/ going for a walk	여행/운동/낚시/산책을 좋아해요.
	yeohaeng/undong/nakssi/sanchag-eul joahaeyo

 .7 Being the host(ess)

See also 4 Eating out

Can I offer you a drink? ____	음료수 드릴까요?
	eumnyosu deurilkkayo?
What would you like to ____ drink?	뭐 마실래요?
	mwo masillaeyo?
Something non-alcoholic,__ please	알콜 성분 없는 것으로 주세요
	alkool seongbun eomneun geoseuro juseyo
Would you like a _____ cigarette/cigar?	담배 드릴까요?
	dambae deurilkkayo?
I don't smoke _____	담배 안 피워요
	dambae an piwoyo
Are you doing anything____ tonight?	오늘 밤에 할 일 있으세요?
	oneul bame halil isseuseyo?
Do you have any plans ____ for today/this afternoon/ tonight?	오늘/오늘 오후/오늘 밤에 무슨 계획 있으세요?
	oneul/oneul ohu/oneul bam-e museun gyehoek isseuseyo?

 .8 Invitations

Would you like to go _____ out with me?	저와 함께 외출 할래요?
	jeowa hamkke oechul hallaeyo?
Would you like to go _____ dancing with me?	저와 함께 춤추러 가실래요?
	jeowa hamkke chumchureo gasillaeyo?
Would you like to have ____ lunch/dinner with me?	저와 함께 점심/저녁 드실래요?
	jeowa hamkke jeomsim/jeonyeok deusillaeyo?
Would you like to come____ to the beach with me?	저와 같이 해변에 가실래요?
	jeowa gachi haebyeone gasillaeyo?
Would you like to come____ into town with us?	우리하고 시내에 가실래요?
	urihago sinaee gasillaeyo?
Would you like to come____ and see some friends with us?	같이 친구 만나러 갈래요?
	gachi chin-gu mannareo gallaeyo?
Shall we dance?_____	춤 추실까요?
	chum chusilkkayo?

- sit at the bar? _____	-바에 앉을까요? *ba.e anjeulkkayo?*
- get something to drink? __	-마실까요? *masilkkayo?*
- go for a walk/drive? _____	-산책하러/드라이브 갈까요? *sanchaekareo/draibeu galkkayo?*
Yes, all right _____	네, 좋아요 *ne, joayo*
Good idea _____	좋은 생각이에요 *joeun saeng-gagieyo*
No thank you _____	고맙지만 사양할께요 *gomapjiman sayanghalkkeyo*
Maybe later _____	나중에요 *najung-eyo*
I don't feel like it _____	별로 내키지 않아요 *byeollo naekiji anayo*
I don't have time _____	시간이 없어요 *sigani eopseoyo*
I already have a date _____	데이트가 있어요 *deiteuga isseoyo*
I'm not very good at dancing/volleyball/ swimming	춤을 잘 못 춰요/ 배구를 잘 못 해요/ 수영 을 잘 못해요 *chumeul jal mot chwoyo/baegureul jal mot haeyo/suyeongeul jal mot haeyo*
You look great _____	근사한데요 *geunsahandeyo*

3.9 Paying a compliment

I like your car _____	차가 참 좋네요 *chaga cham jonneyo*
I like your ski outfit _____	스키 장비가 참 좋네요 *seuki jangbiga cham jonneyo*
You are very nice _____	당신 참 좋은 사람이에요 *dangsin cham joeun saramieyo*
What a good boy/girl! _____	정말 착하군요 *jeongmal chakagunyo*
You're a good dancer _____	춤을 잘 추네요 *chumeul jal chwoneyo*
You're a very good cook __	요리를 아주 잘 하네요 *yorireul aju jal haneyo*
You're a good soccer player	축구를 아주 잘 하네요 *chukgureul aju jal haneyo*
I like being with you _____	당신하고 같이 있는 게 좋아요 *dangsinhago gachi inneun.ge joayo*

3.10 Intimate comments/questions

I've missed you so much	정말 보고 싶었어요 *jeongmal bogo sipeosseoyo*
I dreamt about you _____	당신 꿈을 꿨어요 *dangsin kkumeul kkwosseoyo*
I think about you all day __	하루 종일 당신 생각을 해요 *harujong-il dangsin saeng-gageul haeyo*
I've been thinking about you all day	하루 종일 당신 생각을 했어요 *harujong-il dangsin saeng-gageul haesseoyo*

You have such a sweet ____ 당신은 미소가 정말 아름다워요
  smile *dangsineun misoga jeongmal areumdawoyo*
You have such beautiful ___ 당신은 눈이 정말 아름다워요
  eyes *dangsineun yebbeun nuni jeongmal*
  areumdawoyo
I'm in love with you _____ 당신을 사랑해요
  dangsineul saranghaeyo
I'm in love with you too ___ 나도 당신을 사랑해요
  nado dangsineul saranghaeyo
I love you_____ 당신이 좋아요
  dangsini joayo
I love you too _____ 저도요
  jeodoyo
I don't feel as strongly ____ 당신에 대해 별다른 느낌이 없어요
  about you *dangsine daehae byeoldareun neukkimi*
  eopseoyo
I already have a _____ 전 이미 여자친구/남자친구가 있어요.
  girlfriend/boyfriend *jeon imi yeojachin-gu/namja chin-guga*
  isseoyo.
I'm not ready for that_____ 아직은 안 돼요.
  ajikeun an dwaeyo.
I don't want to rush into it _ 서두르고 싶지 않아요
  seodureugo sipji anayo
Take your hands off me____ 손 대지 말아요
  son daeji marayo
Okay, no problem _____ 그럴께요
  geuleolkkeyo
Will you spend the night___ 같이 밤을 지낼래요?
  with me? *gachi bameul jonaellaeyo?*
I'd like to go to bed with ___ 당신과 자고 싶어요
  you *dangsin.gwa jago sipeoyo*
Only if we use a condom __ 콘돔을 사용한다면요
  kondomeul sayong.handa.myeonyo
We have to be careful _____ 에이즈를 조심해야 해요
  about AIDS *eijeureul josimhaeya haeyo*
That's what they all say____ 그건 사람들이 늘상 하는 말이구요
  geugeon saramdeuli neulsang haneun
  mariguyo
We shouldn't take _____ 위험한 건 안돼요
  any risks *wiheomhan geon an dwaeyo*
Do you have a condom? __ 콘돔 있어요?
  kondom isseoyo?
No? Then the answer's ___ 없으면 안돼요
  no *eopseumyeon an dwaeyo.*

3 .11 Arrangements

When will I see you _____ 언제 다시 만날 수 있나요?
  again? *eonje dasi mannal su innayo?*
Are you free over the _____ 주말에 시간 있어요?
  weekend? *jumare sigan isseoyo?*
What's the plan, then? ____ 무슨 계획이 있어요?
  museun gyehoegi isseoyo?
Where shall we meet? ____ 우리 어디서 만날까요?
  uri eodiseo mannalkkayo?

Conversation

Will you pick me/us up? ___	데리러 올 건가요?
	derireo ol geongayo?
Shall I pick you up? _____	데리러 갈까요?
	derireo galkkayo?
I have to be home by... ____	... 까지는 집에 가야 해요
	...kkajineun jibe gaya haeyo
I don't want to see you ____ anymore	다시 만날 생각 없어요
	disi mannal saenggak eopseoyo
Can I take you home? ____	집에 데려다 줘도 돼요?
	jibe deryeoda jwodo dwaeyo?

3.12 Saying good-bye

Can I write/call you? _____	편지 써도/ 전화 해도 돼요?
	pyeonji sseodo/jeonhwa haedo dwaeyo?
Will you write to me/call me?	편지/전화 해 줄래요?
	pyeonji/ jeonhwa hae jullaeyo?
Can I have your address/ __ phone number?	주소/전화 번호 좀 가르쳐 주세요
	juso/jeonhwa beonho jom gareucheo juseyo
Thanks for everything _____	여러 가지로 고마워요
	yeoreo gagiro gomawoyo
It was a lot of fun _____	즐거웠어요
	jeulgeowosseoyo
Say hello to... _____	... 인사 전해 주세요
	insa jeonhae juseyo
All the best _____	잘 지내세요
	jal jinaeseyo
Good luck _____	행운을 빌어요
	haeng-uneul bireoyo
When will you be _____ back?	언제 돌아오세요?
	eonje doraoseyo?
I'll be waiting for you _____	기다리고 있을게요
	gidarigo isseulkkeyo
I'd like to see you again____	또 봤으면 좋겠어요
	tto bwasseumyeon jokesseoyo
I hope we meet again _____ soon	곧 다시 볼 수 있으면 좋겠어요
	got dasi bol su isseumyeon jokesseoyo
Here's our address, if _____ you're ever in the United States...	우리 주소예요, 미국에 오면...
	uri jusoyeyo, miguge omyeon...
You'd be more than _____ welcome	언제나 환영이에요
	eonjena hwanyeong-ieyo

Eating out

4 Eating out

4 .1 On arrival

I'd like to reserve a table for seven o'clock, please	일곱 시에 예약을 하고 싶은데요 *ilgopsie yeyageul hago sipeundeyo*
A table for two, please	두 사람 테이블 부탁합니다 *dusaram teibeul butakammida*
We've reserved	예약했어요 *yeyak haesseoyo*
We haven't reserved	예약 안 했어요 *yeyak an haesseoyo*
Is the restaurant open yet?	식당이 이미 열었나요? *sikdangi imi yeoreonnayo?*
What time does the restaurant open?	몇 시에 여나요? *myeotsie yeonayo?*
What time does the restaurant close?	몇 시에 닫나요? *myeotsie dannayo?*
Can we wait for a table?	자리를 기다려도 될까요? *jarireul gidaryeoro doelkkayo?*
Do we have to wait long?	오래 기다려야 하나요? *orae gidareoya hanayo?*
Is this seat taken?	이 자리에 누가 있나요? *i jarie nuga innayo?*
Could we sit here/there?	여기/저기 앉아도 될까요? *yeogi/jeogi anjado doelkkayo?*
Can we sit by the window?	창문 쪽에 앉아도 될까요? *changmun jjoge anjado doelkkayo?*
Are there any tables outside?	바깥에도 테이블이 있나요? *bakkatedo teibeuri innayo?*
Do you have another chair for us?	여분의 의자가 있을까요? *yeobunui uijaga isseulkkayo?*
Do you have a highchair?	유아용 의자가 있나요? *yuayong uijaga innayo?*
Is there a socket for this bottle-warmer?	우유병 데울 소켓이 있나요? *uyubyeong deul sokesi innayo?*
Could you warm up this bottle/jar for me?	이 병을 좀 데워주세요 *i byeong.eul jom dewojuseyo*
Not too hot, please	너무 뜨겁지 않게 해 주세요 *neomu tteugeopji anke hae juseyo*

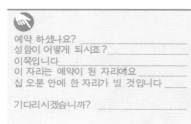

예약 하셨나요?	Do you have a reservation?
성함이 어떻게 되시죠?	What name, please?
이쪽입니다	This way, please
이 자리는 예약이 된 자리얘요	This table is reserved
십 오분 안에 한 자리가 빌 것입니다	We'll have a table free in fifteen minutes
기다리시겠습니까?	Would you like to wait (at the bar)?

Is there somewhere I _____   기저귀 갈아 줄 곳이 있나요?
   can change the baby's   gijeogwi gara jul gosi innayo?
   diaper?
Where are the restrooms? _   화장실은 어디에 있어요?
   hwajangsireun eodie isseoyo?

 .2 Ordering

We'd like something to ____   뭘 좀 먹었으면 / 마셨으면 좋겠어요
   eat/drink   mwol jom meogeosseumyeon/
   masyeosseumyeon jokesseoyo
Could I have a quick meal?_   빨리 되는 음식으로 주세요
   ppalli doeneun eumsigeuro juseyo
We don't have much time__   시간이 별로 없어요
   sigani byeollo eopseoyo
We'd like to have a drink___   음료수 먼저 주세요
   first   eumnyosu meonjeo juseyo
Could we see the menu/ ___   메뉴/포도주 목록을 좀 보여주시겠어요?
   wine list, please?   menyu/podoju mongnogeul jom boyeojuseyo
Do you have a menu in ____   영어로 된 메뉴판이 있나요?
   English?   yeongeoro doen menyupani innayo?
Do you have a dish of the_   오늘의 특별 메뉴/ 여행자용 메뉴가 있나
   day/a tourist menu?   요?
   oneulrui teukbyeol menyu/yeohaengjayong
   menyuga innayo?
We haven't made a choice _   아직 정하지 못했어요
   yet   ajik jeonghaji mothasseoyo
What do you recommend?_   어떤 걸 추천해 주시겠어요?
   eotteon geol chucheonhae jusigesseoyo?
What are the local_____   이 지방의/ 이 식당의 특선요리는 뭐에요?
   specialities/your   i jibang.ui/i sikdang.ui teukseonyorineun
   specialities?   mwoeyo?
I like strawberries/olives ___   딸기/올리브 주세요
   ttalgi/olibeu juseyo
I don't like meat/fish_____   고기는/ 생선은 별로 안 좋아해요
   gogineun/saengseoneun byeollo an joahaeyo
What's this?_____   이게 뭔가요?
   ige mwon.gayo?
Does it have...in it? _____   여기에...이 들어있나요?
   yeogie...i deureoinnayo?
Is it stuffed with...? _____   속에...이 들어있나요?
   soge...i deureoinnayo?
What does it taste like? ____   맛이 어때요?
   masi eoddaeyo?
Is this a hot or a cold _____   이건 따뜻한 요리인가요 차가운 요리인가
   dish?   요?
   igeon ttadeutan yoriin-gayo chagaun yoriin-
   gayo?
Is this sweet? _____   이건 단가요?
   igeon dan-gayo?
Is this hot/spicy? _____   이거 매워요?
   igeo maewoyo?
Do you have anything _____   혹시 다른 것이 있나요?
   else, by any chance?   hoksi dareun geosi innayo?
I'm on a salt-free diet_____   무염식 중이에요
   muyeomsik jung.ieyo

무엇을 드시겠습니까? _____	What would you like?
정하셨어요? _____	Have you decided?
음료를 먼저 드릴까요? _____	Would you like a drink first?
어떤 음료를 드릴까요? _____	What would you like to drink?
...가 모자라요/다 나갔어요 _____	We've run out of...
맛 있게 드세요 _____	Enjoy your meal/Bon appetit
더 필요한 것 있으세요? _____	Is everything all right?
식탁을 치워 드릴까요? _____	May I clear the table?

I can't eat pork _____
돼지 고기를 못 먹어요
dwaeji gogireul mot meogeoyo

I can't have sugar _____
설탕 못 먹어요
seoltang mot meogeoyo

I'm on a fat-free diet _____
무지방 식이요법 중이에요
mujibang sigiyoppeop jungieyo

I can't have spicy food _____
매운 음식을 못 먹어요
maeun-eumsigeul mot meogeoyo

We'll have what those people are having _____
저쪽 사람들이 먹는 걸로 주세요
jeojjok saramdeuri meongneun geollo juseyo

I'd like... _____
... 주세요
...juseyo

We're not having... _____
...은 안 먹을게요
...eun anmeogeulkkeyo

Could I have some more bread, please? _____
빵 좀 더 주세요
ppang jom deo juseyo

Could I have another bottle of water/wine, please? _____
물/포도주 한 병 더 주세요
mul/podoju han byeong deo juseyo

Could I have another portion of..., please? _____
...하나 더 추가해 주세요
...hana deo chugahae juseyo

Could I have the salt and pepper, please? _____
소금하고 후추 주세요
sogeumhago huchu juseyo

Could I have a napkin, please? _____
냅킨 좀 주시겠어요
naepkin jom jusigesseoyo

Could I have a teaspoon, please? _____
차 숟가락 좀 주세요
cha sukkarak jom juseyo

Could I have an ashtray, please? _____
재떨이 좀 주세요
jaetteori jom juseyo

Could I have some matches, please? _____
성냥 좀 주시겠어요
seongnyang jom jusigesseoyo

Could I have some toothpicks, please _____
이쑤시개 좀 주시겠어요
issusigae jom jusigesseoyo

Could I have a glass of water, please _____
물 한 잔 주시겠어요
mul hanjan jusigesseoyo

Could I have a straw please _____
빨대 좀 주세요
ppalttae jom juseyo

Enjoy your meal/Bon appetit _____
식사 맛있게 하세요
siksa masikke haseyo

You too! _____
맛 있게 드세요
masikke deuseyo

Cheers!	건배
	geonbae
The next round's on me ___	다음에는 제가 낼게요
	daeumeneun jega naelkkeyo
Could we have a doggy___ bag, please?	남은 거 좀 싸 주시겠어요
	nameun geo jom ssa jusigesseoyo?

.3 The bill

See also 8.2 Settling the bill

How much is this dish? ____	얼마에요?
	eolmaeyo?
Could I have the bill, _____ please?	계산서 좀 주세요
	gyesanseo jom juseyo
All together	한꺼번에 계산할게요
	hankkeobeone gyesan halkkeyo
Everyone pays separately/ _ let's go Dutch	각자 따로 계산합시다
	gakja ttaro gyesanhapsida
Could we have the menu __ again, please?	메뉴판을 다시 갖다 주세요
	menyupaneul dasi gatda juseyo
The...is not on the bill ____	...가 계산에서 빠졌어요
	...ga gyesaneseo ppajyeosseoyo

.4 Complaints

It's taking a very long____ time	시간이 너무 오래 걸리네요
	sigani neomu orae geollineyo
We've been here an hour _ already	우리가 여기 한 시간이나 있었어요
	uriga yeogi hansiganina isseosseoyo
This must be a mistake ____	뭔가 잘 못 됐네요
	mwon.ga jalmot doeneyo
This is not what I ordered__	이건 제가 주문한 게 아닌데요
	igeon jega jumunhange anindeyo
I ordered...	...를 주문했어요
	...reul jumunhaesseoyo
There's a dish missing ____	요리 한 가지가 빠졌어요.
	yori hangajiga ppajeosseoyo
This is broken/not clean __	이건 부서졌어요/ 이건 깨끗하지 않아요
	igeon buseojeosseoyo/igeon kkaekkeutaji anayo
The food's cold	음식이 식었어요
	eumsigi sigeosseoyo
The food's not fresh _____	음식이 신선하지 않아요
	eumsigi sinseonhaji anayo
The food's too _____ salty/sweet/spicy	이 음식은 너무 짜요/ 너무 달아요/너무 매워요
	i eumsigeun neomu jjayo/neomu darayo/neomu maewoyo
The meat's too rare_____	고기가 너무 덜 익었어요
	gogiga neomu deorigeosseoyo
The meat's overdone _____	고기를 너무 익혔네요
	gogireul neomu ikyeonneyo
The meat's tough _____	고기가 질겨요
	gogiga jilgyeoyo
The meat is off/has gone _ bad	고기가 상했어요
	gogiga sanghaesseoyo

Could I have something ___ else instead of this?	이거 대신 다른 걸로 주세요 *igeo daesin dareun geollo juseyo*
The bill/this amount is ___ not right	계산이 잘 못 됐어요 *gyesani jalmot dwaesseoyo*
We didn't have this ___	이건 안 먹었는데요 *igeon an meogeonneundeyo*
There's no toilet paper in ___ the restroom	화장실에 휴지가 없어요. *hwajangsire hujiga eopseoyo*
Will you call the manager, ___ please?	지배인을 불러주세요. *jibaeineul bulleo juseyo*

.5 Paying a compliment

That was a wonderful ___ meal	맛있게 잘 먹었습니다 *masikke jal meogeosseummida*
The food was excellent ___	음식이 너무 맛있었어요 *eumsigi neomu masisseosseoyo*
The...in particular was ___ delicious	특히...이 맛있네요 *teuki...i masinneyo*

.6 The menu

전채 **starter/hors d'oeuvres**	메인 코스 **main course**	스낵 **snacks**
탕류 **soups**	채식 **vegetable dishes**	음료 **drinks**
면류 **noodles**	전골류 **hot pots**	생선류 **fish**
해산물 **sea food**	서비스 요금 **service charge**	피자 **pizza**
육류 **meat**	어류 **fish**	
닭요리 **poultry**	빵 **bread**	
후식류/ 차 **desserts/tea**	특선요리 **specialties**	
샐러드 **salad**	주류 **liqueur (after dinner)**	
	파스타 **pasta**	

.7 Alphabetcal list of dishes

Korean food is invigorating and varied, with many regions having their own specialities. If you want to taste a variety of dishes in one meal, then try *hanjeongsik*. This set meal usually consists of two types of soup, ten side dishes, and five types of vegetables and fish.

Bibimbap is assorted vegetables on steamed rice with red pepper paste sauce.

Bulgogi is one of the most popular Korean foods. Thin slices of beef are marinated in soy sauce and sesame oil and cooked on a dome-shaped grill.

Galbi (ribs) is another very popular Korean food. The ingredients are as same as for *bulgogi*, but a barbeque grill is used for *galbi*.

Kimchi is an important part of any Korean meal and is made of a spicy mixture of fermented vegetables (most often napa cabbage), chilli, garlic, ginger and other seasonings.

Naengmyeon is the most highly preferred summer dish. It is noodles served with cold beef broth. *Hamheung-naengmyeon,* a variation of *naengmyeon,* is just noodles and hot pepper paste sauce, without broth. There are many places specializing in *naengmyeon* in major cities.

Samgyetang (ginseng chicken soup) is the dish for summer in Korea. Especially on Chobok, Jungbok, and Malbok (days that mark the first, middle and last periods of the summer doldrums), people eat *samgyetang* to beat the summer heat.

Seolleongtang is a beef broth soup with chopped scallions. It is served with rice and it goes very well with *kkakttugi*, radish *kimchi*.

Shinseolo is a delicious mixture of beef and vegetables cooked in a steamboat pot.

Songpyeon are small cakes made of rice-flour dough with a filling of sweetened chestnuts and green mung beans. They are a traditional part of Chuseok, the Korean thanksgiving holiday.

4

Eating out

5

On the road

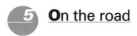

5 On the road

● **In Korea**, cars are driven on the right side of the road and main streets can be very crowded from early morning until late evening. Due to the heavy traffic and often confusing road systems, it may be desirable to hire a driver along with the car, especially in large cities. Travelers who wish to hire a chauffeur-driven car must be prepared to pay the driver's meals and other traveling expenses as well.

Bicycle paths are rare in Korea. Though bikes can be hired in most towns, bikes are not often considered a proper means of transportation on main roads.

5 .1 Asking for directions

Excuse me, could I ask you something?	실례합니다, 뭐 좀 여쭤 볼게요 *sillyehammida, mwo jjom yeojjwobolkkeyo*
I've lost my way	길을 잃었어요 *gireul ireosseoyo*
Is there a ...around here?	이 근처에...가 있나요? *i geuncheoe...ga innayo?*
Is this the way to...?	이쪽이...로 가는 길이 맞나요? *ijjogi...ro ganeun giri mannayo?*
Could you tell me how to get to...?	...로 어떻게 갈 수 있는지 알려주세요 *...ro eotteoke galsu inneunji allyeojuseyo*
What's the quickest way to...?	...로 가는데 제일 빠른 길이 어딘가요? *...ro ganeunde jeil ppareun giri eodin-gayo?*

여기서 어디로 가야 할 지 잘 모르겠어요	I don't know my way around here
길을 잘 못 드셨어요	You're going the wrong way
다시... 쪽으로 돌아가야 해요	You have to go back to...
저기에서부터 표지판을 따라 가세요	From there on just follow the signs
저기 가서 다시 물어보세요	When you get there, ask again

직진 go straight ahead	우회전 turn right	건넘 cross
길/로 the road/street	터널 the tunnel	건물 the building
강 the river	교량 the bridge	교차로 the intersection/ crossroads
좌회전 Turn left	이쪽으로 Follow	길모퉁이에서 at the corner
신호등 the traffic light	양보 the 'yield' sign	화살표 the arrow
고가도로 the overpass	기차 건널목 the grade crossing	

43

How many kilometers _____	...까지 몇 킬로미터인가요?
is it to...?	*...kkaji myeot killomiteo ingayo?*
Could you point it out _____	지도에서 어디인지 가리켜 주세요
on the map?	*jidoeseo eodiinji garikyeo juseyo*

.2 Traffic signs

터널 내 점등	갓길 사용금지	커브
turn on headlights	impassible shoulder	curves
교차로	유료 주차장	위험
intersection/crossroads	paying carpark	danger(ous)
도로 서비스	우측통행/ 좌측통행	접근 금지/ 통행.금지
road assistance	keep right/left	no access/no
(breakdown service)	낙석 주의	pedestrian access
정지	beware, falling rocks	우회
stop	관리자 상근 주차장	detour
인도/보도	supervised	우천시...킬로
sidewalk	garage/parking lot	rain or ice for...kms
일시 주차	도로 통제	우회전/좌회전 금지
parking for a limited	road blocked	no right/left turn
period	차선 변경	파킹 디스크
차량 정비소	change lanes	parking disk
service station	기차 건널목	(compulsory)
방해하지 마시오.	grade crossing	우선권
do not obstruct	스노우 체인 부착	right of way
파손 도로	snow chains	...외 주차 금지
broken/uneven	required	parking reserved
surface	도로 끝	for...
주의/ 조심	road closed	진입 금지
beware	최대 높이	no entry
도로 공사	maximum headroom	서행
road works	출구	slow down
도로 폐쇄	exit	견인지역
road closed	비상시 차선	tow-away area
대형 트럭	emergency lane	통행 금지
heavy trucks	진입로	no passing
통행료	driveway	일방 통행
toll payment	최대 속도	one way
좁아짐	maximum speed	주차금지
road narrows		no parking

.3 The car

See the diagram on page 47

.4 The gas station

How many kilometers to_____	다음 주유소까지는 몇 킬로인가요?
the next gas station,	*daeum juyusokkajineun myeot killoin-gayo?*
please?	
I would like...liters of _____	...리터 넣어주세요
	...riteo neoeojuseyo
super_____	수퍼
	supeo

leaded _____	유연
	uyeon
unleaded _____	무연
	muyeon
diesel _____	디젤
	dijel
...worth of gas _____	...리터 어치
	...riteo eochi
Fill her up, please _____	가득 채워 주세요
	gadeuk chaewojuseyo
Could you check the oil level, please?	오일을 점검해 주세요
	oileul jeomgeomhae juseyo
Could you check the tire pressure, please?	타이어 압력을 점검해 주세요
	taieo amnyeogeul jeomgeomhae juseyo
Could you change the oil, please?	오일을 바꿔주세요
	oileul bakkwojuseyo
Could you clean the windshield, please?	앞 유리를 닦아 주세요
	amnyurireul dakkajuseyo
Could you wash the car, please?	세차 해 주세요
	secha hae juseyo

5 .5 Breakdown and repairs

I've broken down, could you give me a hand?	고장이 났는데, 좀 도와주세요
	gojang-i nanneunde, jom dowajuseyo.
I've run out of gas _____	기름이 다 떨어져가요
	gireumi da tteoreojeogayo
I've locked the keys in the car	열쇠를 두고차 문을 잠갔어요
	yeolsoeleul dugo cha meuneul jamgasseoyo
The car/motorbike/ moped won't start	차/오토바이/모터 자전거가 출발이 안 돼요
	cha/otobai/moteu jajeon-geo-ga chulbari an dweyo
Could you contact the breakdown service for me, please?	수리 서비스 에 연락 좀 해 주세요
	suri seobiseue yeollak jom hae juseyo
Could you call a garage for me, please? .	카 센터에 전화 좀 해 주세요
	ka ssenteoe jeonhwa jom hae juseyo
Could you give me a lift to the nearest garage?	가까운 정비소까지 좀 데려다 주세요
	gakkaun jeongbisokkaji jom deryeoda juseyo
Could you give me a lift to the nearest town?	가까운 시내까지 좀 데려다 주세요
	gakkaun sinaekkaji jom deryeoda juseyo
Could you give me a lift to the nearest telephone booth?	가까운 전화박스까지 좀 데려다 주세요
	gakkaun jeonhwabakseukkaji jom deryeoda juseyo
Could you give me a lift to the nearest emergency phone?	가까운 긴급 전화기 있는 곳에 좀 데려다 주세요
	gakkaun gin-geup jeonhwagi inneungose jom deryeoda juseyo
Can we take my moped?	제 모터 자전거를 가지고 가도 돼요?
	je moteujajeon-georeul gajigo gado dwaeyo?
Could you tow me to a garage?	정비소까지 견인해 주세요
	jeongbisoekkaji gyeoninhae juseyo
There's probably something wrong with...(See pages 46-47)	...에 문제가 있는 것 같아요
	...e munjega inneun geot gatayo
Can you fix it? _____	고칠 수 있나요?
	gochil su innayo?

The parts of a car
(the diagram shows the numbered parts)

1	battery	배터리	*baeteori*
2	rear light	미등	*mideung*
3	rear-view mirror	백미러	*baekmireo*
	backup light		*bakeop rait*
4	aerial	안테나	*antena*
	car radio	카 라디오	*ca radio*
5	gas tank	연료 탱크	*yeollyo taenk*
6	spark plugs	스파크 플러그	*spakeu peulleogeu*
	fuel pump	연료 펌프	*yeollyo peompeu*
7	side mirror	사이드 미러	*saideu mireo*
8	bumper	범퍼	*beompeo*
	carburettor	카뷰레터/ 기화기	*cabyureteo/gihwagi*
	crankcase	크랭크 케이스	*keurangk keiseu*
	cylinder	실린더	*sillindeo*
	ignition	시동	*sidong*
	warning light	경보등	*gyeongbodeung*
	generator	제너레이터	*jeneoraiteo*
	accelerator	액셀러레이터/ 가속장치	*aekselleorateo/ gasok jangchi*
	handbrake	핸드브레이크	*haend breikeu*
	valve	밸브	*baelbeu*
9	muffler	소음기	*soeumgi*
10	trunk	트렁크	*teureongkeu*
11	headlight	해드라이트/ 전조등	*haedraiteu/ jeonjodeung*
	crank shaft	크랭크 축	*kraenk chuk*
12	air filter	에어 필터	*eeo pilteo*
	fog lamp	안개등	*an-gaedeong*
13	engine block	엔진 블록	*enjin beullok*
	camshaft	캠축	*kaemchuk*
	oil filter/pump	오일필터/ 펌프	*oil pilteo/peompeu*
	dipstick	오일 스틱	*oil seutik*
	pedal	페달	*pedal*
14	door	도어	*doeo*
15	radiator	냉각기	*naeng-gakki*
16	brake disc	브레이크 디스크	*breikeu diseukeu*
	spare wheel	스페어 바퀴	*speeo bakkwi*
17	indicator	계기판	*gyegipan*
18	windshield	앞 유리	*amnyuri*
	wiper	와이퍼	*waipeo*
19	shock absorbers	쇼크 업저버/ 충격 흡수체	*sokeu eopseeobeo/ chung-gyeok heupsuche*
	sunroof	선루프	*seonrup*
	spoiler	스포일러	*seupoilleo*
20	steering column	스티어링 컬럼	*seutieoring keolleom*
	steering wheel	핸들	*haendeul*
21	exhaust pipe	배기관	*baegigwan*
22	seat belt	안전 벨트	*anjeon belteu*
	fan	팬/ 환풍기	*pan/hwanpung-gi*
23	distributor	배전기	*baejeon-gi*
	cables	케이블	*keibeul*
24	gear shift	기어	*gieo*

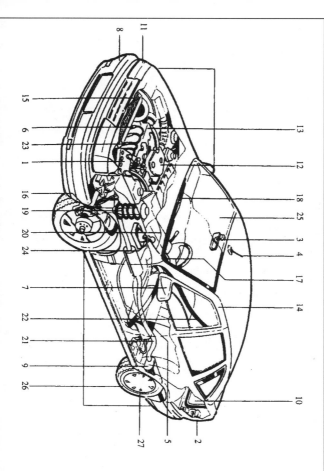

	water pump	워터 펌프	*woteo peompeu*
25	wheel	바퀴	*bakwi*
26	hubcap	휠캡	*wilkaep*
	piston	피스톤	*piseuton*

Could you fix my tire? _____	타이어를 좀 고쳐 주세요
	taieoreul gochyeojuseyo
Could you change this_____ wheel?	이 바퀴를 바꿔 주세요
	i bakwireul bakkwo juseyo
Can you fix it so it'll _____ get me to...?	...까지 갈 수 있도록 고칠 수 있어요?
	...kkaji gal su ittorok gochil su isseoyo?
Which garage can help _____ me?	어떤 정비소로 가면 되나요?
	eoddeon jeongbisoro gamyeon doenayo?
When will my car/_____ bicycle be ready?	차/ 자전거 수리가 언제까지 될까요?
	cha/jajeon-geo suriga eonjekkaji doelkkayo?
Have you finished yet? _____	벌써 끝내셨어요?
	beolsseo kkeunnaesyeosseoyo?
Can I wait for it here?_____	여기서 기다려도 될까요?
	yeogiseo gidaryeodo doeyo?
How much will it cost? _____	얼마 정도가 들까요?
	eolmajeongdoga deulkkayo?
Could you itemize the _____ bill?	청구서에 항목별로 써 주세요
	cheong-guseoe hangmokbyeollo sseo juseyo
Could you give me a _____ receipt for insurance purposes?	보험 처리 할 영수증을 주세요
	boheom cheorihal yeongsujeung-eul juseyo

5 .6 The motorcycle/bicycle

See the diagram on page 51

● **Bicycle paths** are common in towns and cities and their use is strongly recommended. Bikes can usually be rented at tourist centers. The maximum speed for mopeds is 40 km/h both inside and outside town centers. Crash helmets are compulsory.

손님 차/ 자전거 부품이 없습니다 _____	I don't have parts for your car/bicycle
다른 곳에서 부품을 가져 와야 해요 _____	I have to get the parts from somewhere else
부품을 주문해야 해요 _____	I have to order the parts
반나절 걸릴 거예요 _____	That'll take half a day
하루 정도 걸릴 거예요 _____	That'll take a day
며칠 걸릴 거예요 _____	That'll take a few days
일 주일 걸릴 거예요 _____	That'll take a week
차가 완전히 망가졌네요_____	Your car is a write-off
고칠 수 없어요 _____	It can't be repaired
차/ 오토바이/ 모터 자전거/자전거를... _____ 시에 찾으러 오세요	The car/motorcycle/moped/ bicycle will be ready at ...o'clock

⑤ .7 Renting a vehicle

● **To rent a car**, a driver should have more than one year's experience, an international driver's license, a passport and should be over 21 years old.

I'd like to rent a..._____	...를 빌리고 싶은데요
	...reul billigo sipeundeyo
Do I need a (special)_____ license for that?	이걸 쓰려면 (특수) 면허증이 필요한가요?
	igeol sseuryeomyeon (teuksu) myeonheojjeung-i piryohangayo?
I'd like to rent the...for... ___	...를...에 쓰려고 빌리고 싶어요
	...reul...e sseuryeogo billigo sipeoyo
the...for a day _____	...를 하루 빌리고 싶어요
	...reul haru billigo sipeoyo
the...for two days _____	...를 이틀간 빌리고 싶어요
	...reul iteulgan billigo sipeoyo
How much is that per_____ day/week?	하루/ 일 주일에 얼마인가요?
	harue/iljuire eolmain-gayo?
How much is the deposit? _	예치금은 얼마인가요?
	yechigeumeun eolmain-gayo?
Could I have a receipt ____ for the deposit?	예치금 영수증을 받을 수 있나요?
	yechigeum yeongsujeung-eul badeulsu innayo?
How much is the _____ surcharge per kilometer?	킬로 당 추가 요금은 얼마인가요?
	killodang chuga yogeumeun eolmain-gayo?
Does that include gas?_____	기름도 포함하고 있나요?
	gireumdo pohamhago innayo?
Does that include _____ insurance?	보험도 되나요?
	boheomdo doenayo?
What time can I pick_____ the...up?	...를 몇 시에 가지러 오면 되나요?
	...reul myeot sie gajireo omyeon doenayo?
When does it have to_____ be back?	언제까지 반납해야 하나요?
	eonjekkaji bannaphaeya hanayo?
Where's the gas tank? _____	기름탱크는 어디에 있나요?
	gireum taenkeuneun eodie innayo?
What sort of fuel does ____ it take?	어떤 연료를 쓰나요?
	eotteon yeollyoreul sseunayo?

⑤ .8 Hitchhiking

● **Hitchhiking** is very rare in Korea. Getting a ride from a stranger may be difficult, but these are some common directions and courtesies.

Where are you heading? ___	어디 가요?
	eodi gayo?
Can you give me a lift? ____	태워 주시겠어요?
	taewo jusigesseoyo?
Can my friend come too? __	제 친구도 타도 돼요?
	je chin-gudo tado dwaeyo?
I'd like to go to... _____	...에 가고 싶은데요
	...e gago sipeundeoyo
Is that on the way to...? ____	...로 가는 길이세요?
	...ro ganeun giriseyo?
Could you drop me off...? __	...에 좀 내려 주세요
	...e jom naeryeo juseyo
Could you drop me off _____ here?	여기서 좀 내려주세요
	yeogiseo jom naeryeo juseyo

On the road

The parts of a motorcycle/bicycle
(the diagram shows the numbered parts)

1	rear light	미등	*mideung*
2	rear wheel	뒷 바퀴	*dwitbakwi*
3	(luggage) carrier	바구니	*baguni*
4	bell	벨	*bel*
	inner tube	튜브	*tyubeu*
	tire	타이어	*taieo*
5	peddle crank	페달축	*pedal chuk*
6	gear change	기어	*gieo*
	wire	와이어	*waieo*
	generator	제너레이터	*geneoreiteo*
	frame	프레임	*preim*
7	wheel guard	휠 가드	*hwil gadeu*
8	chain	체인	*chein*
	chain guard	체인 가드	*chein gadeu*
	odometer	주행계	*juhaeng-gye*
	child's seat	아동용 의자	*adong-yong uija*
9	headlight	전조등	*jeonjodeung*
	bulb	벌브	*beolb*
10	pedal	페달	*pedal*
11	pump	펌프	*peompeu*
12	reflector	반사경	*bansagyeong*
13	brake shoe	브레이크	*breikeu*
14	brake cable	브레이크 케이블	*breikeu keibeul*
15	anti-theft device	도난 방지 장치	*donan bangji jangchi*
16	carrier straps	소품걸이	*sopumgeoli*
	tachometer	스피드 미터	*seupideu miteo*
17	spoke	스포크	*seupokeu*
18	mudguard	진흙받이	*jinheuk baji*
19	handlebar	손잡이	*sonjabi*
20	chain wheel	체인	*chein*
	toe clip	발 고정기	*bal gojeoong-gi*
21	crank axle	크랭크	*keuraengkeu*
	drum brake	드럼 브레이크	*deureom beureikeu*
22	rim	틀	*teul*
23	valve	밸브	*baelbeu*
24	gear cable	기어 케이블	*gieo keibeul*
25	fork	포크 케이블	*pokeu keibeul*
26	front wheel	앞 바퀴	*ap bakwi*
27	seat	의자	*uija*

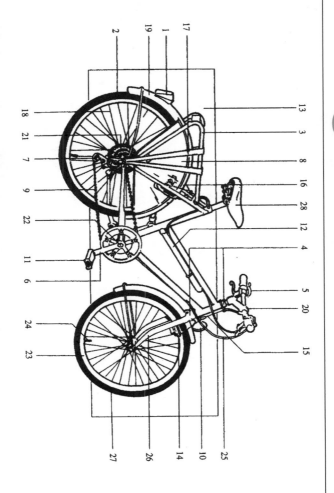

Could you drop me off at __ 고속도로 진입할 때 좀 내려주세요
the entrance to the *gosokdoro jinniphalttae jom naeryeo juseyo*
highway?
Could you drop me off ____ 센터에 좀 내려주세요
in the center? *senteoe jom naeryeo juseyo*
Could you drop me off ____ 다음 교차로에서 좀 세워 주세요
at the next intersection? *daeum gyocharoeseo jom sewo juseyo*
Could you stop here, _____ 여기에 좀 세워 주세요
please? *yeogie jom sewo juseyo*
I'd like to get out here ____ 여기서 내려 주세요
yeogie naeryeo juseyo
Thanks for the lift _____ 태워 주셔서 감사합니다
taewo jusyeoseo gamsahammida

5

On the road

6

Public transportation

Public transportation

● **There are eight subway lines** in Seoul, each indicated by a different color. They link the farthest parts of Seoul and its satellite cities and transfers between lines may be made at various stations. Trains operate at intervals of 2.5 to 3 minutes during the morning and evening rush hours, and at intervals of 4 to 6 minutes during the rest of the day.

There are three kinds of urban buses running in Seoul: City, City Express and Deluxe Express. The City Express buses (*jwaseok*) are more comfortable than City buses (*ilban*). There is a further type of bus (*maeul*) that is a kind of a shuttle bus: it runs over short distances in residential areas that lack convenient transportation such as the subway or regular buses. Usually these buses are smaller and cheaper than the normal buses. Since the transportation card is not yet valid for these buses, fares have to be paid in cash.

You may get assistance from your hotel front desk to find out where the bus stops are and which number you need to take. You may also contact the Bus Route Information Center.

.1 In general

(...시)...행 기차가...분까지(정도) 연착되고 있습니다	The [time] train to...has been delayed by (about)...minutes
지금...행 기차가 승강장에 도착하고 있습니다	The train to...is now arriving
...발 기차가 승강장에 들어오고 있습니다	The train from...is now arriving
다음 역은 ... 입니다.	The next station is...

Where does this train go to?	이 기차는 어디로 가나요? *i gichaneun eodiro ganayo?*
Does this boat go to...?	이 배는 ... 로 가나요? *i baeneun ...ro ganayo?*
Can I take this bus to...?	...로 가려면 이 버스를 타면 되나요? *...ro garyeomyeon i beoseureul tamyeon doenayo?*
Does this train stop at...?	이 기차가 ...에 서나요? *i gichaga ...e seonayo?*
Is this seat taken/free/ reserved?	이 자리에 누가 있습니까?/빈자리 입니까?/예약된 자리인가요? *i jarie nuga isseummikka?/ binjari immikka?/ yeoyakdoen jariin-gayo?*
I've reserved...	...를 예약했는데요. *...reul yeyakhaenneundeoyo*
Could you tell me where I have to get off for... ?	...로 가려면 어디에서 내리면 되나요? *...ro gayeomyeon eodieseo naerimyeon doenayo?*
Could you let me know when we get to...?	...에 도착하면 알려 주세요. *...e dochakhamyeon allyeojuseyo*

Could you stop at the next stop, please?	다음 역에 세워 주세요 *daeum nyeoge sewojuseyo*
Where are we?	여기가 어딘가요? *yeogiga eodin-gayo?*
Do I have to get off here?	여기에서 내려야 하나요? *yeogieseo naeryeoya hanayo?*
Have we already passed...?	벌써...를 지나쳤어요? *beolsseo ...reul jinachyeosseoyo?*
How long have I been asleep?	제가 잠을 얼마나 잤나요? *jega jameul eolmana jannayo?*
How long does the train stop here?	기차가 여기에 얼마동안 멈출까요? *gichaga yeogie eolmattong-an meomchulkkayo?*
Can I come back on the same ticket?	돌아갈 때 같은 표를 쓰면 되나요? *doragalttae gateun pyoreul sseumyeon doenayo?*
Can I change on this ticket?	이 표로 갈아탈 수 있나요? *i pyoro garatalsu innayo?*
How long is this ticket valid for?	이 표는 유효기간이 얼마동안 인가요? *i pyoneun yuhyogigani eolmattong-an in-gayo?*
How much is the extra fare for the high speed train?	고속열차를 타려면 추가 비용이 얼마인가요? *gosong.yeolchareul taryeomyeon chuga biyong-i eolmain-gayo?*

6.2 Customs

여권 주세요	Your passport, please
영주권 보여 주세요	Your green card, please
자동차 등록서류 주세요	Your vehicle documents, please
사증/비자 보여주세요	Your visa, please
어디로 가나요?	Where are you going?
얼마동안 머물 계획인가요?	How long are you planning to stay?
신고할 것이 있습니까?	Do you have anything to declare?
이것 열어주세요	Open this, please

My children are entered on this passport	우리 아이들은 이 여권으로 들어왔어요 *uri aideureun i yeokkwoneuro deureowasseoyo*
I'm traveling through...	...로 여행할 거에요 *...ro yeohaeng-halgeoyeyo*
I'm going on vacation to...	...로 휴가 갈 거에요 *...ro huga galgeoyeyo*
I'm on a business trip	출장 중이에요 *chuljjang jung-ieyo*
I don't know how long I'll be staying	얼마나 머무를지 아직 모르겠어요 *eolmana meomureuljji ajik moreugesseoyo*
I'll be staying here for a weekend	여기에 주말동안 머물 거에요 *yeogie jumaldong-an meomul geoeyo*

Public transportation

I'll be staying here for a few days	여기에 며칠동안 머물 거에요
	yeogie myeochildong-an meomul geoeyo
I'll be staying here a week	여기 일 주일 머물 거에요
	yeogie iljuil meomul geoeyo
I'll be staying here for two weeks	여기 이 주일 머물 거에요
	yeogie ijuil meomul geoeyo
I've got nothing to declare	신고할 것이 없어요
	sin-gohal geosi eopsseoyo
I have...	...가 있어요
	...ga isseoyo
a carton of cigarettes	담배 한 보루
	dambae han boru
a bottle of...	...한 병
	...han byeong
some souvenirs	기념품
	ginyeompum.
These are personal items	이건 개인 물건이에요
	igeon gaein mulgeonieyo
These are not new	이건 새 것이 아니에요
	igeon saegeosi anieyo
Here's the receipt	영수증 여기 있어요
	yeongsujeung yeogi isseoyo
This is for private use	이건 개인 용도로 산 거에요
	igeon gaein yongdoro sangeoeyo
How much import duty do I have to pay?	수입관세를 얼마나 내야 하나요?
	suip gwansereul eolmana naeya hanayo?
May I go now?	이제 가도 되나요?
	ije gado doenayo?

6 .3 Luggage

Porter!	여기요!
	yeogiyo!
luggage to...?	이 짐을...로 옮겨주세요
	i jimeul...ro omgyeojuseyo
How much do I owe you?	얼마를 드리면 되나요?
	eolmareul deurimeun doenayo?
Where can I find a cart?	카트는 어디에 있나요?
	kateuneun eodie innayo?
Could you store this luggage for me?	이 짐을 좀 보관해 주세요
	i jimeul jom bogwanhae juseyo
Where are the luggage lockers?	물품 보관소는 어디에 있나요?
	mulpum bogwansoneun eodie innayo?
I can't get the locker open	보관함을 열 수가 없어요
	bogwanhameul yeolsuga eopsseoyo
How much is it per item per day?	하루에 한 품목 당 얼마인가요?
	harue han pummok-dang eolmaingayo?
This is not my bag/suit case	이건 제 가방/서류 가방이 아닌데요
	igeon je gabang/seoryu gabang-i anindeyo
There's one item/bag/ suitcase missing	한 개/가방/서류 가방이 없어졌어요
	han gae/gabang/seoryu gabang-i eopseojyeosseoyo
My suitcase is damaged	제 서류 가방에 손상이 생겼어요
	je seoryu gabang-e sonsang-i saeng-gyeosseoyo

56

Ticket types

일등석/ 이등석	First/second class
편도/ 왕복	Single/return
흡연/ 금연	Smoking/non-smoking
창가 쪽 좌석	Window seat
앞 쪽/ 뒤 쪽	Front/back (of train)
좌석/ 침대	Seat/berth
위/ 가운데/ 아래	Top/middle/bottom
일반석/ 일등석	Economy/first class
선실/ 좌석	Cabin/seat
일인용/ 이인용	Single/double
몇 명이세요?	How many are traveling?

Destination

어디로 가나요?	Where are you traveling?
언제 떠나나요?	When are you leaving?
...는...시에 출발합니다	Your...leaves at...
...를 바꿔야 해요	You have to change
...에서 내려야 해요	You have to get off at...
...를 통해서/ 경유해서 가야 해요	You have to go via....
...(일)에 출발해요	The outward journey is on...
...(일)에 도착해요	The return journey is on...
...시까지는 타야/탑승해야 합니다	You have to be on board by....(o'clock)

Inside the vehicle

표 주세요	Tickets, please
예약(표) 주세요	Your reservation, please
여권 주세요	Your passport, please
다른 자리에 앉으셨어요	You're in the wrong seat
뭔가 실수를 한 것 같은데요/ ... 를 잘 못 한 것 같은데요	You have made a mistake/You are in the wrong...
여기는 예약이 된 자리예요	This seat is reserved
추가 비용을 내야 해요	You'll have to pay extra
...가...분 연착되고 있습니다	The...has been delayed by...minutes

.5 Tickets

Where can I...?	...는 어디에서 하면 되나요?
	...neun eodieseo hamyeon doenayo?
- buy a ticket?	표는 어디에서 팔아요?
	pyoneun eodieseo parayo?
- reserve a seat?	좌석은 어디에서 예약하면 되나요?
	jwaseogeun eodieseo yeyakhamyeon doenayo?
- reserve a flight?	비행기 표는 어디에서 예약하면 되나요?
	bihaeng-gipyoneun eodieseo yeyakhamyeon doenayo?
Could I have...for...please?	...행...를 주세요
	...haeng ...reul juseyo
A single to...please	...행 편도 한 장 주세요
	...haeng pyeondo hanjang juseyo
A return ticket, please	왕복 한 장 주세요
	wangbok hanjang juseyo
first class	일등석
	iltteungseok
second class	이등석
	iltteungseok
economy class	일반석
	ilbanseok
I'd like to reserve a seat/berth/cabin	좌석/침대/선실을 예약하고 싶은데요
	jwaseok/chimdae/seonsilreul yeyakhago sipeundeyo
I'd like to reserve a top/middle/bottom berth in the sleeping car	침대차 위/가운데/아래 침대를 예약하고 싶은데요
	chimdaecha wi/gaunde/arae chimdaereul yeyakhago sipeundeyo
smoking/non-smoking	흡연/ 금연
	heubyeon/geumyeon
by the window	창가 쪽
	chang-ga jjok
single/double	일인석/ 이인석
	irinseok/iinseok
at the front/back	앞 쪽/ 뒤쪽
	apjjok/dwijjok
There are...of us	...명 있어요
	...myeong isseoyo
We have a car	차가 있어요
	chaga isseoyo
We have a trailer	트레일러가 있어요
	teureilleoga isseoyo
We have...bicycles	자전거...대를 가지고 있어요
	jajeon-geo...daereul gajigo isseoyo
Do you have a...?	...가 있나요?
	...ga innayo?
- weekly travel card?	주 정기권 있어요?
	ju jeong-gikkwon isseoyo
- monthly season ticket?	월 정기권 있어요?
	wol jeong-gikkwon isseoyo?
Where's...?	...는 어디 있나요?
	...neun eodi innayo?
Where's the information desk?	안내소는 어디에 있나요?
	annaesoneun eodie innayo?

Public transportation

Where can I find a _____ schedule?	운행시간표는 어디 있나요? *unhaengsiganpyoneun eodi innayo?*
Where's the...desk? _____	...소는 어디 있나요? *...soneun eodi innayo?*
Do you have a city map_____ with the bus/the subway routes on it?	버스/지하철 노선 지도가 있나요? *beoseu/jihacheol noseon jidoga innayo?*
Do you have a schedule? __	운행시간표 가지고 있나요? *unhaengsiganpyo gajigo innayo?*
Will I get my money back? _	환불해 주나요? *hwanbul hae junayo?*
I'd like to confirm/cancel/ __ change my reservation for/trip to...	...행 예약을 확인/취소/변경하고 싶은데요 *...haeng yeyageul hwagin/chwiso/byeon-gyeong hago sipeundeyo*
I'd like to go to... _____	...에 가고 싶은데요 *...e gago sipeundeyo*
What is the quickest _____ way to get there?	거기까지 가는 제일 빠른 길이 어딘가요? *geogikkaji ganeun jeil ppareun giri eodin-gayo?*
How much is a _____ single/return to...?	...행 편도/왕복표 값은 얼마예요? *...haeng pyeondo/wangbokpyo gapseun eolmayeyo?*
Do I have to pay extra? _____	추가 비용을 내야 하나요? *chuga biyong-eul naeya hanayo?*
Can I break my journey _____ with this ticket?	이 표로 중간에 내렸다 다시 탈수 있어요? *i pyoro jung-gane naeryeotda dasi talsu isseoyo?*
How much luggage am I___ allowed?	짐은 얼마까지 돼요? *jimeun eolmakkaji dwaeyo?*
Is this a direct train? _____	이건 직행인가요? *igeon jikhaeng in-gayo?*
Do I have to change? _____	갈아 타야 돼요? *gara taya dwaeyo?*
Where? _____	어디에서요? *eodieseoyo?*
Does the plane stop _____ anywhere?	비행기가 어디에 들르나요? *bihaeng-giga eodie deulleunayo?*
Will there be any _____ stopovers?	어디 경유해서 가요? *eodi gyeong-yuhaeseo gayo?*
Does the boat stop at any___ other ports on the way?	이 배는 가다가 어디 들러요? *i baeneun gadaga eodi deulleoyo?*
Does the train/bus stop _____ at...?	이 기차/ 버스가...에 서요? *i gicha/beoseuga ...e seoyo?*
Where do I get off? _____	어디서 내려요? *eodiseo naeryeoyo?*
Is there a connection to...? _	...로 가는 연결편이 있나요? *...ro ganeun yeon-gyepyeoni innayo?*
How long do I have to _____ wait?	얼마나 기다려야 해요? *eolmana gidaryeoya haeyo?*
When does...leave?_____	...가 언제 떠나요? *...ga eonje tteonayo?*
What time does the _____ first/next/last...leave?	첫/다음/마지막...는 몇 시에 떠나요? *cheot/daeum/majimak ...neun myeot sie tteonayo?*

How long does...take? _____	...는 얼마나 걸리나요?
	...neun eolmana geollinayo?
What time does it arrive ____ in...?	...에 몇 시에 도착해요?
	...e myeot sie dochakhaeyo?
Where does the...to...leave _ from?	...행...가 어디서 출발해요?
	...haeng...ga eodiseo chulbarhaeyo?
Is this the train/bus...to...?__	...로 가는 기차/버스 있나요?
	...ro ganeun gicha/beoseu innayo?

6.7 Airplanes

● **On arrival** at one of Korea's many international and domestic airports, you will find the following signs:

체크 인	국제선	국내선
check-in	international	domestic flights
도착	출발	
arrivals	departures	

6.8 Trains

● **Korea** is well-served by an extensive network of express and local trains operated by the Korean National Railroad. Special package tours are available for foreign travelers and prices vary for first class, standard class and sleeping cars.

6.9 Taxis

임대	빈 차	택시 승차장
for hire	not occupied	taxi stand

Taxi! _____	택시!
	taeksi!
Could you get me a taxi, ___ please?	택시 좀 불러 주세요
	taeksi jom bulleo juseyo
Where can I find a taxi_____ around here?	이 근처 어디에서 택시를 잡을 수 있나요?
	i geuncheo eodieseo taeksireul jabeulsu innayo?
Could you take me to..., ___ please?	...까지 데려다 주세요
	...kkaji deryeoda juseyo
to this address _____	까지 갑니다
	kkaji gammida
to the...hotel _____	...호텔까지 가요
	... hotelkkaji gayo
to the town/city center_____	시내에 가 주세요
	sinaee ga juseyo
to the station _____	역에 갑니다
	yeoge gammida
to the airport, please _____	공항에 가요
	gonghang-e gayo
How much is the trip to...? _	...까지 얼마예요?
	...kkaji eolmayeyo?

How far is it to...?	...까지 얼마나 먼가요?
	...kkaji eolmana meon-gayo?
Could you turn on the meter, please?	미터기 올려 주세요
	miteogi ollyeo juseyo
I'm in a hurry	좀 급해요
	jom geuphaeyo
Could you speed up/slow down a little?	좀 더 빨리/천천히 가 주세요
	jom deo ppalli/cheoncheonhi ga juseyo
Could you take a different route?	다른 길로 가 주세요
	dareun gillo gajuseyo
I'd like to get out here, please	여기 세워 주세요
	yeogi sewo juseyo
Go...	...갑시다
	...gapsida
You have to go...here	여기서...가야 해요
	yeogiseo...gayahaeyo
Go straight ahead	앞으로 똑바로 가세요
	apeuro ddokbaro gaseyo
Turn left	좌회전이요
	jwahwoejeoniyo
Turn right	우회전이요
	uheojeoniyo
This is it/We're here	다 왔어요
	da wasseoyo
Could you wait a minute for me, please?	잠시만 기다려 주세요
	jamsiman gidaryeo juseyo

Public transportation

Overnight accommodation

Overnight accommodation

7.1 **G**eneral

얼마나 오래 계실 건가요?	How long will you be staying?
이 용지를 작성해 주세요	Fill out this form, please
여권 좀 보여주세요	Could I see your passport?
예차금이 필요해요	I'll need a deposit
선불로/ 미리 지불해야만 합니다	You'll have to pay in advance

My name is...	제 이름은... 입니다
	je ireumeun...immida
I've made a reservation	예약을 했어요
	yeyageul haesseoyo
How much is it per night/week/ month?	하룻밤/ 한 주/ 한 달에 얼마인가요?
	harutbam/han ju/han dar-e eolmain-gayo?
We'll be staying at least...nights/weeks	여기에 적어도...일/주 머물 거에요
	yeogie jeogeodo...chil/ju meomulkkeoeyo
We don't know yet	아직 잘 모르겠어요
	ajik jal moreugesseoyo
Do you allow pets?	애완동물도 허용되나요?
	aewandongmuldo heoyongdoenayo?
What time does the door open/close?	몇 시에 문을 여세요/닫으세요?
	myeotsie muneul yeoseyo/dadeuseyo?
Could you get me a taxi, please?	택시를 불러 주세요
	taeksireul bulleo juseyo
Is there any mail for me?	저한테 온 우편물 있나요?
	jeohante on upyeonmul innayo?

7 .2 **C**amping/backpacking

See the diagram on page 65

야영지를 직접 고를 수 있어요	You can pick your own site
야영지를 배정할 거에요	You'll be allocated a site
이게 야영지 번호 입니다	This is your site number
이것을 손님 차에 단단히 붙여 주세요	Please stick this firmly to your car
이 카드를 잃어버리면 안 됩니다	You must not lose this card

Where's the manager?	매니저는 어디에 있나요?
	maenijeoneon eodie innayo?
Are we allowed to camp here?	여기에 야영해도 되나요?
	yeogie yayeonghaedo doenayo?
There are...of us and we have...tents	...명과 텐트...개가 있습니다
	...myeong-gwa tenteu ...gaega itsseummida

Overnight accommodation

Camping/backpacking equipment

(the diagram shows the numbered parts)

	luggage space	수화물 보관소	*suhwamul bogwanso*
	can opener	병따개	*byeongttagae*
	butane gas	부탄 가스	*butan gaseu*
	bottle	병	*byeong*
1	pannier	짐 바구니	*jimbbaguni*
2	gas cooker	가스 요리기구	*gaseu yorigigu*
3	hammer	망치	*mangchi*
	hammock	그물 침대	*geumul chimdae*
4	gas can	가스 용기	*gaseu yong-gi*
	campfire	캠프파이어/모닥불	*kaemp-paieo/modakbul*
5	folding chair	접이 의자	*jeobi uija*
6	ice pack	얼음 주머니	*eoreum jumeoni*
	compass	나침반	*nachimban*
	corkscrew	코르크 마개 뽑이	*koreukeu magae ppobi*
7	airbed	공기 침대	*gonggi chimdae*
8	airbed pump	공기침대 펌프	*gonggi chimae peompeu*
9	awning	천막	*cheonmak*
10	sleeping bag	침낭	*chimnang*
11	saucepan	냄비/ 소스팬	*naembi/soseupaen*
12	handle (pan)	손잡이 냄비	*sonjabi naembi*
	lighter	라이터/ 점화기	*raiteo/jeomhwagi*
13	backpack	배낭	*baenang*
14	rope	로프	*ropeu*
15	storm lantern	전등	*jeondeung*
	camp bed	야영 침대	*yayeong chimdae*
	table	탁자	*takja*
16	tent	텐트/ 천막	*tenteu/chunmak*
17	tent peg	천막 말뚝	*chunmak malttuk*
18	tent pole	천막 기둥	*chunmak gidung*
	thermos	보온병	*boonppyeong*
19	water bottle	물병	*mulppyeong*
	clothes pin	빨래집게	*ppallaejipge*
	clothes line	빨래 줄	*ppallaejjul*
	windbreak	바람 막이	*baram-magi*
20	flashlight	손전등	*sonjeondeung*
	penknife	주머니칼	*jumeoni kal*

Overnight accommodation

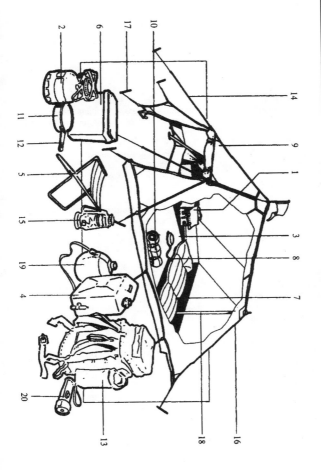

Can we pick our own site?	우리가 야영지를 직접 골라도 되나요? *uriga yayeong-jireul jikjeop gollado doenayo?*
Do you have a quiet spot for us?	좀 조용한 곳을 찾는데요 *jom joyonghan goseul channeundeyo*
Do you have any other sites available?	다른 데에 빈 곳이 있나요? *dareun dee bin gosi innayo?*
It's too windy/sunny/ shady here	여긴 바람이 너무 불어요/ 햇볕이 심해요/ 그늘이 져요 *yeogin barami neomu bureoyo/ haetbyeochi simhaeyo/ geuneuri jyeoyo*
It's too crowded here	여긴 너무 복잡해요 *yeogin neomu bokjaphaeyo*
The ground's too hard/uneven	땅이 너무 단단해요./ 울퉁불퉁해요 *ttang-i neomu dandanhaeyo./ultungbultung haeyo*
Do you have a level spot for the camper/trailer/ folding trailer?	야영/이동주택/ 조립주택으로 사용할 수 있는 평평한 곳이 있나요? *yayeong/idongjutaek/ joripjutaegeuro sayonghalsu inneun pyeongpyeonghan gosi innayo?*
Could we have adjoining sites?	붙어있는 곳으로 주세요 *buteoinneun goseuro juseyo*
Can we park the car next to the tent?	텐트 옆에 차를 세워도 되나요? *tenteu yeope chaeul sewodo doenayo?*
How much is it per person/tent/car?	일인당/ 한 텐트 당 / 차 한대 당 얼마인가요? *irindang/han tenteu dang/ cha handae dang eolmain-gayo?*
Do you have chalets for hire?	임대 중인 별장이 있나요? *imdae jung.in byeoljjang-i innayo?*
Are there any...?	...가 있나요? *...ga innayo?*
Are there any hot showers?	온수가 나오는 샤워실이 있나요? *onsuga naoneun syawosiri innayo?*
Are there any washing machines?	세탁기가 있나요? *setakgiga innayo?*
Is there a...on the site?	야영지에 ... 가 있나요? *yayeong-jie ...ga innayo?*
Is there a children's play area on the site?	야영지에 놀이터가 있나요? *yayeong-jie noriteoga innayo?*
Are there covered cooking facilities on the site?	야영지에 요리시설이 있나요? *yayeong-jie yorisiseori innayo?*
Can I rent a safe?	금고를 빌리고 싶은데요 *geumgoreul billigo sipeundeyo*
Are we allowed to barbecue here?	바비큐 파티를 해도 되나요? *babikyu patireul haedo doenayo?*
Are there any power outlets?	전선 꽂을 데가 있어요? *Jeonseon kkojeul dega isseoyo?*
Is there drinking water?	식용수가 있나요? *sigyongsuga innayo?*
When's the garbage collected?	쓰레기는 언제 치워가나요? *sseuregineun eonje chiwoganayo?*
Do you sell gas bottles (butane gas/ ropane gas)?	가스통(부탄 가스/프로판 가스) 팔아요? *gaseutong (butan gaseu/peuropan gaseu) parayo?*

Overnight accommodation

Do you have a single/ _____ 일인용/이인용 빈 방 있나요?
  double room available? *irinyong/iinyong binbang innayo?*
per person/per room _____ 일인당/ 방 하나 당
  irindang/ bang hanadang

Does that include _____ 아침/점심/저녁 식사도 포함되나요?
  breakfast/lunch/ *achim/jeomsim/jeonyeok siksado*
  dinner? *pohamdoenayo?*
Could we have two_____ 붙어 있는 방으로 두 개 주세요
  adjoining rooms? *buteo inneun bang-euro dugae juseyo*
with/without toilet/ _____ 화장실/욕실/샤워실이 있는/없는
  bath/shower *hwajangsil/yoksil/syawosiri inneun/eomneun*
facing the street_____ 길쪽으로 향하는
  giljjogeuro hwanghaneun

at the back_____ 뒤쪽에
  dwijjoge

with/without sea view _____ 바다 경치가 보이는/보이지 않는
  bada gyeongchiga boineun/boiji anneun

Is there...in the hotel?_____ 호텔에...가 있나요?
  hotere ...ga innayo?

Is there an elevator in _____ 호텔에 승강기/엘리베이터가 있나요?
  the hotel? *hotere seung-gang-gi/ellibeiteoga innayo?*
Do you have room _____ 룸서비스 되나요?
  service? *rum seobiseu doenayo?*
Could I see the room? _____ 방을 볼 수 있을까요?
  bang-eul bolsu isseulkkayo?

I'll take this room_____ 이 방으로 할게요.
  i bang-euro halkkeyo?

We don't like this one _____ 이건 마음에 들지 않네요
  igeon maeume deulji anneyo

Do you have a larger/less __ 좀 더 비싼/ 싼 방이 있나요?
  expensive room? *jom deo bissan/ssan bang-i innayo?*
What time's breakfast? ____ 아침 식사는 몇 시 인가요?
  achimsiksaneun myeotsi-in-gayo?

Where's the dining room? _ 식당은 어디에 있나요?
  sikdang-eun eodie innayo?

Can I have breakfast in my_ 제 방에서 아침을 먹어도 되나요?
  room? *je bang-eseo achimeul meogeodo doenayo?*
Where's the emergency_____ 비상구/화재 대피구는 어디인가요?
  exit/fire escape? *bisang-guneun/hwajae daepiguneun eodi-in-
  gayo?*
Where can I park my car ___ 차는 어디에 주차하면 되나요?
  safely? *chaneun eodie juchahamyeon doenayo?*
The key to room..., please _ ....호실 열쇠 주세요
  ...hosil yeolsoe juseyo
Could you put this in the___ 이걸 보관해 주세요
  safe, please? *igeol bogwanhaejuseyo*

화장실과 샤워실은 같은 층에/ _____	The toilet and shower are on
실내에 있습니다 _____	the same floor/in the room
이쪽으로 오세요 _____	This way please
손님의 방은...층, ...호실입니다 _____	Your room is on the...floor,
	number...

Overnight accommodation

7

Could you wake me at...tomorrow?	내일...시에 깨워 주세요 *naeil ...sie kkaewojuseyo*
Could you find a babysitter for me?	아이 봐 줄 사람을 찾아봐 주세요 *ai bwa jul saramrul chajabwa juseyo*
Could I have an extra blanket?	여분의 담요가 필요해요 *yeobunui damnyoga piryohaeyo*
What days do the cleaners come in?	청소하러 무슨 요일에 오나요? *cheongsohareo museun yoire onayo?*
When are the sheets/ towels/dish towels changed?	시트/수건/행주는 언제 갈아주나요? *siteu/sugeon/haengjuneun eonje garajunayo?*
We can't sleep for the noise	시끄러워서 잠을 잘 수가 없어요 *sikkeureowoseo jameul jalsuga eopseoyo*

.4 Complaints

Could you turn the radio down, please?	라디오 소리를 좀 낮춰 주세요 *radio sorireul jom nachwojuseyo*
We're out of toilet paper	화장실 휴지를 다 써 가요 *hwajangsil hyujireul da sseo gayo*
There aren't any.../there's not enough...	...가 없어요./모자라요 *...ga eopseoyo./mojarayo*
The bed linen's dirty	침대 요가 지저분해요 *chimdaeyoga jijeobunhaeyo*
The room hasn't been cleaned	방이 깨끗하지가 않아요 *bang-i kkaekkeuthajiga anayo*
The kitchen is not clean	부엌이 깨끗하지 않아요 *bueogi kkaekkeuthaji anayo*
The kitchen utensils are dirty	부엌 용구가 지저분해요 *bueok yong-guga jijeobunhaeyo*
The heating isn't working	난방이 안 되요 *nabang-i andoeyo*
There's no (hot) water/ electricity	(뜨거운) 물이 안 나와요/ 전기가 안 들어와요 *(tteugeoun) muri annawayo/jeon-giga an deureowayo*
...doesn't work/is broken	...가 안 되요./ 고장 났어요 *...ga andoeyo/gojang nasseoyo*
Could you have that seen to?	이것 손 봐주세요 *igeot son bwa juseyo*
Could I have another room/site?	다른 방/곳을 주세요 *dareun bang/goseul juseyo*
The bed creaks terribly	침대가 심하게 삐걱거려요 *chimdaega simhage ppigeok-georyeoyo*
The bed sags	침대가 내려 앉았어요. *chimdaega naryeo anjasseoyo*
Could I have a board under the mattress?	매트리스 밑에 판을 대 주세요 *maeteuriseu mite paneul dae juseyo*
It's too noisy	너무 시끄러워요 *neomu sikkeureowoyo*
There are a lot of insects/bugs	벌레가 너무 많아요 *beollaega neomu manayo*
This place is full of mosquitoes	여긴 모기가 너무 많아요 *yeogin mogiga neomu manayo*
This place is full of cockroaches	여긴 바퀴벌레가 너무 많아요 *yeogin bakwibeollaega neomu manayo*

Overnight accommodation

.5 Departure

See also 8.2 Settling the bill

I'm leaving tomorrow	내일 떠날 예정입니다
	naeil tteonal yejeong-immida
Could I pay my bill, please?	요금 계산하고 싶은데요
	yogeum gyesanhago sipeundeyo
What time should we check out?	몇 시에 체크아웃 하면 되나요?
	myeotsie chekeuaut hamyeon doenayo?
Could I have my deposit/passport back, please?	예치금/여권을 돌려 주세요
	yeochigeum/yeokkwoneul dollyeo juseyo
We're in a big hurry	지금 너무 급해요
	jigeum neomu geuphaeyo
Could you forward my mail to this address?	제 우편물을 이 주소로 보내주세요
	je upyeonmureul i jusoro bonaejuseyo
Could we leave our luggage here until we leave?	떠날 때까지 짐을 여기 둬도 되나요?
	tteonalddaekkaji jimeul yeogi dwodo doenayo?
Thanks for your hospitality	친절하게 대해 주셔서 감사합니다
	chinjeolhage daehae jusyeoseo gamsahammida

Overnight accommodation

Money matters

8

8 Money matters

8.1 Banks

Where can I find a bank around here?	은행이 이 근처 어디에 있어요? *eunhaeng-i i geuncheo eodie isseoyo?*
Where can I cash this traveler's check?	여행자 수표는 어디서 바꿀 수 있나요? *yeohaengja supyoneun eodiseo bakkulsu innayo?*
Can I cash this...here?	여기서 이...바꿀 수 있어요? *yeogiseo i...bakkulsu isseoyo?*
Can I withdraw money on my credit card here?	제 신용 카드로 현금인출이 되나요? *je sinyong kadeuro hyeon.geum inchuri doenayo?*
What's the minimum/ maximum amount?	최소 /최대 한도액이 얼마예요? *choeso/choedae handoaegi eolmayeyo?*
Can I take out less than that?	그것보다 적게 인출도 되나요? *geugeotboda jeokge inchuldo doenayo?*
I had some money cabled here	여기로 얼마 송금을 했어요 *yeogiro eolma song-geumeul haesseoyo*
Has it arrived yet?	벌써 받았나요? *beolsseo badannayo?*
These are the details of my bank in the US	이건 미국에 있는 제 은행에 대한 세부 내용 입니다 *igeon miguge inneun je eunhaeng-e daehan sebu naeyong.immida*
This is the number of my bank account	이게 제 은행 계좌 번호 입니다 *ige je eunhaeng gyeojwa beonhoimmida*
I'd like to change some money	돈을 좀 바꾸고 싶은데요 *doneul jom bakkugo sipeundeyo*
I'd like to change...pounds	파운드를...로 바꾸고 싶은데요 *paundeureul ...ro bakkugo sipeundeyo*
I'd like to change...dollars	달러를...로 바꾸고 싶은데요 *dalleoreul ...ro bakkugo sipeundeyo*
What's the exchange rate?	환율이 어떻게 되나요? *hwanyuri eotteotke doenayo?*
Could you give me some small change with it?	이걸 잔돈으로 좀 바꿔주세요 *igeol jandoneuro bakkwo juseyo*
This is not right	이건 맞지가 않는데요 *ingeon matjiga anneundeyo*

여기 서명해 주세요	Sign here, please
이거 작성해 주세요	Fill this out, please
여권을 보여 주세요	Could I see your passport, please?
신분증을 보여 주세요	Could I see your identity card, please?
은행 카드를 보여 주세요	Could I see your bank card, please?

8 .2 Settling the bill

Could you put it on my _____ bill?	제 계산서에 포함시켜 주시겠어요? *je gyesanseoe pohamsikyeo jusigesseoyo?*
Is the tip included? _____	팁도 포함되나요? *tipdo pohamdoenayo?*
Can I pay by...?_____	...로 계산하고 싶은데요 *...ro gyesanhago sipeundeyo*
Can I pay by credit card?___	신용카드로 계산할게요 *sinyong kadeuro gyesanhalkkeyo*
Can I pay by traveler's _____ check?	여행자 수표로 계산해도 되나요? *yeohaengja supyoro gyesangaedo doenayo?*
Can I pay with foreign _____ currency?	외국환으로 계산해도 되나요? *oegukhwaneuro gyesanhaedo doenayo?*
You've given me too _____ much/you haven't given me enough change	거스름돈을 너무 많이 주셨어요./ 잔돈을 덜 주셨네요 *geoseureum doneul neomu mani jusyeosseoyo./jandoneul deol jusyeonneyo*
Could you check this _____ again, please?	이거 다시 체크 해 주실래요? *igeo dasi chekeu hae jusillaeyo?*
Could I have a receipt, _____ please?	영수증 주세요 *yeongsujeung juseyo*
I don't have enough _____ money on me	돈이 좀 모자라는데요 *doni jom mojaraneundeyo*
This is for you _____	여기 있습니다 *yeogi isseummida*
Keep the change _____	잔돈은 그냥 가지세요 *jandoneun geunyang gajiseyo*

신용카드/ 여행자 수표/외국 돈은 받지 않습니다.	We don't accept credit cards/traveler's checks/foreign currency

Mail and telephone

Mail and telephone

● **With the popularization** of the Internet, a number of Internet cafes and so-called 'PC rooms' have appeared everywhere in Korea. There, people enjoy surfing on the sea of information or playing games with other netizens around the world, along with snacks and music.

Post offices in Korea have been diversifying their business areas. A variety of banking services are now available at more than 3,000 post offices across the nation. They also operate mail order services and issue some civil affairs documents.

Mailing services are divided mainly into two kinds: speed delivery and ordinary delivery. Speed delivery mail arrives within 1-2 days for about double the postal rates, while ordinary mail arrives within 2-4 days.

9.1 Mail

우표	전보	우편환
stamps	telegrams	money orders
소포		
parcels		

Where is...?	...어디에 있어요?
	...eodie isseoyo?
Where is the nearest post office?	가까운 우체국 어디에 있어요?
	gakkaun uchegugi eodie isseoyo?
Where is the main post office	중앙 우체국이 어디에 있어요?
	jung-ang uchegugi eodie isseoyo?
Where is the nearest mail box?	가까운 우체통이 어디에 있어요?
	gakkaun uchetong-i eodie isseoyo?
Which counter should I go to?	어느 창구로 가면 되나요?
	eoneu chang-guro gamyeon doenayo?
Which counter should I go to to send a fax?	팩스를 보내려면 어느 창구로 가면 되나요?
	pakseureul bonaeryeomyeon eoneu chang-guro gamyeon doenayo?
Which counter should I go to to change money?	돈을 바꾸려면 어느 창구로 가면 되나요?
	doneul bakkuryeomyeon eoneu chang-guro gamyeon doenayo?
Which counter should I go to to send giro checks?	지로를 보내려면 어느 창구로 가면 되나요?
	jiroreul bonaeryeomyeon eoneu chang-guro gamyeon doenayo?
Which counter should I go to to wire a money order?	송금하려면 어느 창구로 가면 되나요?
	song-geumharyeomyeon eoneu chang-guro gamyeon doenayo?
Which counter should I go to for general delivery?	일반 우편은 어느 창구로 가면 되나요?
	ilban upyeon baedareun eoneu chang-guro gamyeon doenayo?
Is there any mail for me?	제게 온 우편있어요?
	jege on upyeon isseoyo?
My name's...	제 이름은... 입니다
	je ireumeun...immida

Stamps

What's the postage for_____ ...to...?	...을...로 보내는데 얼마 들어요? *...eul...ro bonaeneunde eolmadeureoyo?*
Are there enough stamps __ on it?	이 우표로 충분해요? *i upyoro chungbunhaeyo?*
I'd like [value] [quantity] __ stamps	[value] 짜리 우표 [quantity] 장 주세요 *...jjari upyo...jang juseyo*
I'd like to send this _____	이것을 보내려고 하는데요 *igeoseul bonaeryeogo haneundeyo*
I'd like to send this _____ express	이걸 빠른우편으로 보내려고 하는데요 *igeol ppareun upyeoneuro bonaeryeogo haneundeyo*
I'd like to send this by air __ mail	이걸 항공우편으로 보내려고 하는데요 *igeol hang-gong upyeoneuro bonaeryeogo haneundeyo*
I'd like to send this by _____ registered mail	이걸 등기로 보내려고 하는데요 *igeol deung-giro bonaeryeogo haneundeyo*

Telegram/fax

I'd like to send a telegram _ to...	...로 전보를 보내려고 하는데요 *...ro jeonboreul bonaeryeogo haneundeyo*
How much is that per_____ word?	한 자에 얼마예요? *han jae eolmayeyo?*
This is the text I want to ___ send	이것을 전보로 보내려고 해요 *igeoseul jeonboro bonaeryeogo haeyo*
Shall I fill out the form_____ myself?	제가 써 넣어야 하나요? *jega sseo neoeoya hanayo?*
Can I make photocopies/___ send a fax here?	여기서 복사/팩스 할 수 있어요? *yeogiseo boksa/paekseu halsu isseoyo?*
How much is it per page?__	한 페이지에 얼마예요? *han peijie eolmayeyo?*

 .2 Telephone

See also 1.8 Telephone alphabet

● **Direct international calls** can easily be made from public telephones using a phone card available from newspaper stands or from vending machines next to the telephone booths. Phone cards have a value of 2,000 or 3,000 Won. Dial 001 or 002 to get out of Korea, then the relevant country code (USA 1), city code and number.

Is there a phone booth _____ around here?	근처에 공중전화 있어요? *geuncheo-e gongjung jeonhwa isseoyo?*
May I use your phone,_____ please?	전화 좀 써도 될까요? *jeonhwa jom sseodo doelkkayo?*
Do you have a phone_____ directory?	전화 번호부 가지고 계세요? *jeonhwa beonhobu gajigo gyeseyo?*
Where can I get a phone___ card?	전화카드를 어디서 사나요? *jeonhwa kadeureul eodiseo sanayo?*
Could you give me...? _____	...좀 가르쳐 주세요 *... jom gareucheo juseyo*

Mail and telephone

Could you give me the ____ number for international directory assistance?	국제전화 안내번호를 좀 가르쳐 주세요 *gukje jeonhwa annaebeonhoreul jom gareucheo juseyo*
Could you give me the ____ number of room...?	...실 전화 번호를 좀 가르쳐 주세요 *...sil jeonhwa beonhoreul jom gareucheo juseyo*
Could you give me the ____ international access code?	국제자동전화 식별번호를 좀 가르쳐 주세요 *gukje jadongjeonhwa sikbyeol beonhoreul jom gareucheo juseyo*
Could you give me the ____ country code?	국가 번호를 좀 가르쳐 주세요 *gukka beonhoreul jom gareucheo juseyo*
Could you give me the ____ area code?	지역 번호를 좀 가르쳐 주세요 *jiyeok beonhoreul jom gareucheo juseyo*
Could you give me the ____ number of [subscriber]...?	...의 번호를 좀 가르쳐 주세요 *...ui beonhoreul jom gareucheo juseyo*
Could you check if this ____ number's correct?	번호가 맞는 지 확인 좀 해 주세요 *beonhoga manneunji hwagin jom hae juseyo*
Can I dial international____ direct?	국제 직통 전화를 할 수 있나요? *gukje jiktong jeonhwareul hal su innayo?*
Do I have to go through ____ the switchboard?	교환을 불러야 되나요? *gyohwaneul bulleoya doenayo?*
Do I have to dial '0' first? ____	0 번을 먼저 눌러야 하나요? *yeongbeoneul meonjeo nulleoya hanayo?*
Do I have to reserve my ____ calls?	전화기록을 남겨둬야 하나요? *jeonhwa girogeul namgyeodwoya hanayo?*
Could you dial this _____ number for me, please?	이 번호로 전화 좀 해 주실 수 있어요? *i beonhoro jeonhwa jom hae jusilsu isseoyo?*
Could you put me through _ to extension..., please?	...번으로 연결해 주세요 *...beoneuro yeongyeolhae juseyo*
I'd like to place a collect ____ call to...	...에게 콜렉트 콜을 하려고 해요 *...ege kollekt koreul haryeogo haeyo*
What's the charge per ____ minute?	일 분에 얼마예요? *ilbune eolmayeyo?*
Have there been any calls_ for me?	제게 전화 온 거 있어요? *jege jeonhwa on geo isseoyo?*

The conversation

Hello, this is..._____	여보세요, ...입니다 *yeoboseyo, ...immida*
Who is this, please? _____	누구세요? *nuguseyo?*
Is this...? _____	...이세요? *...iseyo?*
I'm sorry, I've dialed_____ the wrong number	죄송합니다, 잘 못 걸었어요. *joesong.hammida, jal mot georeosseoyo*
I can't hear you _____	잘 안 들리는 데요 *jal an deullineundeyo*
I'd like to speak to... _____	...좀 바꿔 주세요 *... jom bakkwo juseyo*
Is there anybody who _____ speaks English?	영어를 할 줄 아는 분이 계세요? *yeongeoreul hal juraneun buni gyeseyo?*
Extension..., please_____	...번으로 연결해 주세요 *...beoneuro yeongyeol hae juseyo*
Could you ask him/her to _ call me back?	...에게 전화해 달라고 전해주세요 *ege jeonhwa hae dallago jeonhae juseyo*

My name's... _____ 제 이름은 ... 입니다
je ireumeun ... immida

My number's... _____ 제 전화번호는...입니다
je jeonhwa beonhoneun ...immida

Could you tell him/her I____ 제가 전화했다고 전해주세요
  called? *jega jeonhwa haetdago jeonhae juseyo*

I'll call him/her back _____ 내일 다시 전화할게요
  tomorrow *naeil dasi jeonhwa halkeyo*

전화가 왔었습니다 _____	There's a phone call for you
0 번을 먼저 누르세요 _____	You have to dial '0' first
잠깐 기다리세요_____	One moment, please
응답이 없습니다_____	There's no answer
통화 중입니다_____	The line's busy
기다리시겠어요?_____	Do you want to hold?
연결 중입니다_____	Connecting you
잘 못 거셨습니다_____	You've got a wrong number
자리에 없습니다_____	He's/she's not here right now
잠시 후 돌아오실 겁니다 _____	He'll/she'll be back later
...의 자동 응답기입니다 _____	This is the answering machine of...

Mail and telephone

9

Shopping

10

10 **S**hopping

● **Most shops** in Korea are open for long hours. Major department stores are open from 10:30 a.m. until 7:30 p.m. including Sundays, but smaller shops are usually open until late evening every day. There are also 24-hour convenience stores available in major cities. You can converse in English in the shopping arcades of major hotels and certainly in Itaewon Market, which is located in Southern Seoul. Shops in Namdaemun Market and Dongdaemun Market in Seoul offer a variety of goods at bargain prices.

식품점 grocery shop	시계점 watches and clocks	음반가게 music shop (CDs, tapes, etc)
빨래방 coin-operated laundry	가구점 furniture shop	생선가게 fishmonger
청과물상 fruit and vegetable shop	중고상 second-hand shop	빵집 bakery
이발관 barbers	안경점 optician	가전제품 household appliances
서점 book shop	옷가게 clothing shop	닭 파는 집 poultry shop
장난감가게 toy shop	빵집 baker's shop	청과물상 greengrocer
인조 보석 costume jewelry	신문 가판대 newsstand	향수전문점 perfumery
정육점 butcher's shop	등산장비점 camping supplies shop	아이스크림가게 ice cream shop
악기점 musical instrument shop	미용실 hairdresser	델리가게 delicatessen
신발가게 footwear	카메라점 camera shop	보석상 jeweler
오토바이/자전거 수리점 motorbike/bicycle repairs	사탕/케이크 전문점 confectioners/cake shop	슈퍼마켓 supermarket
철물점 hardware shop	한의원 herbalist's shop	백화점 department store
구두수선 shoe repair	운동구점 sporting goods	담배가게 tobacconist
시장 market	가죽전문점 leather goods	미용실 beauty salon
금세공 goldsmith	약국 pharmacy	화원 nursery (plants)
문구점 stationery shop	이불가게 household linen shop	유제품가게 dairy (shop selling dairy products)
포목점 fabric shop	모피전문점 furrier	세탁소 laundry
	꽃집 florist	

.1 Shopping conversations

Where can I get...?	... 어디에 있어요?
	... eodie isseoyo?
When is this shop open?	이 가게 몇 시까지 열어요?
	i gage myot sikkaji yeoreoyo?
Could you tell me where the ... department is?	... 매장 어디에 있어요?
	... maejang eodie isseoyo?
Could you help me, please?	여기 좀 봐 주시겠어요?
	yeogi jom bwa jusigesseoyo?
I'm looking for ...	... 찾고 있는데요
	... chatgo inneundeyo
Do you sell English/ American newspapers?	영자 신문 있어요?
	yeongja sinmun isseoyo?

도와 드릴까요?	**Are you being served?**

No, I'd like...	아뇨, ...고 싶어요
	anyo, ...go sipeoyo
I'm just looking, if that's all right	그냥 구경하는 중이에요
	geu-nyang gu.gyeonghaneun jung.ieyo

또 필요하신 거 없으세요?	**Anything else?**

Yes, I'd also like ...	네, ...도 주세요
	ne, ...do juseyo
No, thank you. That's all	아뇨, 괜찮아요. 그게 전부예요
	anyo, gwaenchanayo. geuge jeonbuyeoyo.
Could you show me ...?	... 좀 보여 주시겠어요?
	... jom boyeo jusigesseoyo?
I'd prefer ...	...가 더 좋아요.
	...ga deo joayo
This is not what I'm looking for	이거 제가 찾는 거 아니예요
	igeo jega channeun geo aniyeoyo
Thank you, I'll keep looking	감사합니다, 좀 더 구경하겠어요
	gamsahamnida, jom deo gugyeunghagesseoyo
Do you have something ...?	...거 있어요?
	...geo isseoyo?
less expensive?	덜 비싼
	deol bissan
smaller?	더 작은
	deo jageun
larger?	더 큰
	deo keun
I'll take this one	이거 사겠어요
	igeo sagesseoyo
Does it come with instructions?	설명서도 같이 있나요?
	seolmyeongseodo gachi innayo?
It's too expensive	너무 비싸요
	neomu bissayo

Shopping

10

I'll give you ... _____	... 드리겠어요
	... deurigesseoyo
Could you keep this for _____ me?	이거 좀 보관해 주시겠어요?
	igeo jom bogwanhae jusigesseoyo?
I'll come back for it later _____	나중에 가지러 오겠어요
	najung-e gajireo ogesseoyo
Do you have a bag for _____ me, please?	쇼핑백 하나 주시겠어요?
	syopingbaek hana jusigesseoyo?
Could you gift wrap it, _____ please?	이거 선물포장 좀 해 주시겠어요?
	igeo seonmulpojang jom hae jusigesseoyo?

죄송합니다, 없습니다 _____	I'm sorry, we don't have that
죄송합니다, 매진입니다 _____	I'm sorry, we're sold out
죄송합니다, ... 까지는 안 들어옵니다 _____	I'm sorry, it won't come back in until...
계산대에서 지불하세요 _____	Please pay at the cash register
신용카드 안 받습니다 _____	We don't accept credit cards
여행자 수표 안 받습니다 _____	We don't accept traveler's checks
외국돈 안 받습니다 _____	We don't accept foreign currency

🔟 .2 Food

I'd like a hundred grams _____ of ..., please	... 백그람 주세요
	... baek geuram juseyo
I'd like half a kilo/five _____ hundred grams of ...	... 반 키로/... 오백그람 주세요
	... ban kiro/... obaekgeuram juseyo
I'd like a kilo of... _____	... 일키로 주세요
	... ilkiro juseyo
Could you ... it for me, _____ please?	... 좀 주시겠어요?
	... jom jusigesseoyo?
slice it/cut it up for me, _____ please?	썰어/잘라 주시겠어요?
	sseoreo/jalla jusigesseoyo?
grate it for me, please? _____	갈아 주시겠어요?
	gara jusigesseoyo?
Can I order it?_____	주문할 수 있어요?
	jumun hal su isseoyo?
I'll pick it up tomorrow/ _____ at ...	내일/... 시에 가지러 오겠어요
	naeil/... sie gajireo ogesseoyo
Can you eat/drink this? _____	이거 먹을 수/마실 수 있어요?
	igeo meogeul su/masil su isseoyo?
What's in it? _____	그 안에 뭐가 들었어요?
	geu ane mwoga deureosseoyo?

🔟 .3 Clothing and shoes

I saw something in the _____ window	쇼 윈도우에서 뭘 좀 봤어요
	syo windoueseo mwol jom bwasseoyo
Shall I point it out? _____	가리켜 드릴까요?
	garikye deurilkkayo?

I'd like something to go____ with this	이거하고 어울리는 걸 사고싶어요 *igeohago eoullineun geol sago sipeoyo*
Do you have shoes to ____ match this?	이거하고 어울리는 신발 있어요? *igeohago eoullineun sinbal isseoyo?*
I'm a size ... in the US ____	미국식으로 사이즈 ... 이에요 *miguksigeuro saijeu ... ieyo*
Can I try this on? _____	이거 입어(clothing)/ 신어(shoes)봐도 돼요? *igeo ibeo(clothing)/sineo(shoes) bwado dwaeyo?*
Where's the fitting room? __	탈의실이 어디에 있어요? *tarisili eodie isseoyo?*
It doesn't suit me_____	저에게 안 맞아요 *jeoege an majayo*
This is the right size _____	이게 맞는 사이즈예요 *ige manneun saijeuyeyo*
It doesn't look good on ____ me	저에게 안 어울려요 *jeoege an eoullyeoyo*
Do you have this/these ____ in ...(size, color)?	이거 ...로 있어요? *igeo ...ro isseoyo?*
The heels too high/low ____	굽이 너무 높아요/ 낮아요 *gubi neomu nopayo/najayo*
Is this real leather? _____	이거 진짜 가죽이에요? *igeo jinjja gajugieyo?*
I'm looking for a ... for ____ a ...-year-old child	(age)... 살짜리 어린이용 (goods)...을/를 찾고 있어요 *(age)... saljjari eoriniyong (goods)...eul/reul chatgo isseoyo*
I'd like a ... _____	...을/를 사고 싶어요 *...eul/reul sago sipeoyo*
silk _____	실크 *silkeu*
cotton _____	면 *myeon*
woolen _____	울 *ul*
linen _____	린넨 *rinnen*
At what temperature _____ should I wash it?	몇 도에 세탁해야 해요? *myeotdoe setakaeya haeyo?*
Will it shrink in the wash?__	세탁 후에 줄어들어요? *setak hue jureodeureoyo?*

손 세탁 **Hand wash**	다리지 마세요. **Do not iron**	탈수기로 짜지 마세요 **Do not spin dry**
드라이 클리닝 **Dry clean**	기계세탁 가능 **Machine washable**	뉘어서 말리세요 **Lay flat**

At the cobbler

Could you mend these____ shoes?	이 구두 좀 고쳐 주시겠어요? *i gudu jom gochyeo jusigesseoyo?*
Could you resole/reheel ___ these shoes?	이 구두 밑창/굽 좀 갈아 주시겠어요? *i gudu mitchang/gup jom gara jusigesseoyo?*
When will they be ready? __	언제 될까요? *eonje doelkkayo?*

I'd like..., please _____ ... 좀 주세요
                              ... jom juseyo
a can of shoe polish _____ 구두약 한 통
                              guduyak han tong
a pair of shoelaces _____ 구두끈 한 벌
                              gudukkeun han beo

10 .4 Photographs and video

I'd like a film for this_____ 이 카메라에 맞는 필름 하나 주세요
  camera, please   i kamere manneun pilleum hana juseyo
I'd like a cartridge, please _ 카트릿지 하나 주세요
                              kateuritji hana juseyo
a one twenty-six _____ 스물여섯 장 짜리 카트릿지 하나 주세요.
  cartridge, please   seumulyeoseot jang jjari kateuritji hana
                              juseyo
a slide film_____ 슬라이드용 필름 하나
                              seullaideuyong pilleum hana
a movie cassette _____ 영화용 필름 하나
                              yeonghwayong pilleum hana
a videotape _____ 비디오 테이프 하나
                              bidio teipeu hana
color/black and white_____ 칼라/흑백
                              kalla/heukbaek
super eight _____ 수퍼 에이트
                              supeo eiteu
12/24/36 exposures _____ 열두 장/스물네 장/서른여섯 장 짜리
                              yeoldu jang/seumulne jang/seoreunyeoseot
                              jang jjari
ASA/DIN number_____ 에이에스에이/ 디아이엔 넘버
                              eieseuei/diaien neombeo

Problems

Could you load the film ____ 필름 좀 넣어 주시겠어요?
  for me, please?   pilleum jom neo-eo jusigesseoyo?
Could you take the film ____ 필름 좀 꺼내 주시겠어요?
  out for me, please?   pilleum jom kkeonae jusigesseoyo?
Should I replace the _____ 밧데리를 갈아야 합니까?
  batteries?   batderireul garaya hamnikka?
Could you have a look at __ 제 카메라 좀 봐 주시겠어요?
  my camera, please?   je kamera jom bwa jusigesseoyo?
It's not working _____ 작동이 안 돼요
                              Jadong-i an dwaeyo
The ... is broken_____ ...이/가 고장났어요
                              ...i/ga gojangnasseoyo
The film's jammed _____ 필름이 꽉 끼었어요
                              pilleumi kkwak kkieosseoyo
The film's broken_____ 필름이 끊어졌어요
                              pilleumi kkeuneojyeosseoyo
The flash isn't working ___ 플래쉬가 안돼요
                              peullaeswiga an dwaeyo

Processing and prints

I'd like to have this film ____ developed/printed, please	이 필름 현상/인화 좀 해 주세요 *i pilleum hyeonsang/inhwa jom hae juseyo*
I'd like ... prints from ____ each negative	전부 ... 장씩 뽑아주세요 *jeonbu ... jangssik ppoba juseyo*
glossy/matte ____	광택지/매트지 *gwangtaekji/maeteuji*
6 x 9 ____	육 구 인치 사이즈 *yuk gu inchi saijeu*
I'd like to order reprints ____ of these photos	이 사진 좀 더 뽑아 주세요 *i sajin jom deo ppoba juseyo*
I'd like to have this photo ____ enlarged	이 사진 좀 확대 해 주세요 *I sajin jom hwakdae hae juseyo*
How much is processing? ____	뽑는 데 얼마예요? *ppomneun de eolmayeyo?*
How much for printing? ____	인화하는 데 얼마예요? *inhwahaneun de eolmayeyo?*
How much are the ____ reprints?	더 뽑는 데 얼마예요? *deo ppomneun de eolmayeyo?*
How much is it for ____ enlargement?	확대하는 데 얼마예요? *hwakdaehaneun de eolmayeyo?*
When will they be ready? ____	언제 될까요? *eonje doelkkayo?*

10 .5 At the hairdresser's

Do I have to make an ____ appointment?	예약해야 돼요? *yeyakhaeya dwaeyo?*
Can I come in right now? ____	지금 당장 가도 돼요? *jigeum dangjang gado dwaeyo?*
How long will I have to ____ wait?	얼마동안 기다려야 될까요? *Eolmadong-an gidaryeoya doelkkayo?*
I'd like a shampoo/haircut ____	샴푸/ 컷트 좀 해 주세요. *syampu/keoteu jom hae juseyo.*
I'd like a shampoo for ____ oily/dry hair, please	지성/ 건성 머리용 샴푸 좀 해 주세요 *jiseong/geonseong meoriyong syampu jom hae juseyo*
I'd like an anti-dandruff ____ shampoo	비듬 샴푸 좀 해 주세요 *bideum syampu jom hae juseyo*
I'd like a color-rinse ____ shampoo, please	염색전용 샴푸 좀 해 주세요 *yeomsaekjeonyong syampu jom hae juseyo*
I'd like a shampoo with ____ conditioner, please	린스겸용 샴푸 좀 해 주세요. *rinseugyeomyong syampu jom hae juseyo*
I'd like highlights, please ____	블리치 좀 넣어주세요 *beullichi jom neo-eo juseyo*
Do you have a color ____ chart, please?	칼라 견본 있어요? *kalla gyeonbon isseoyo?*
I'd like to keep the same ____ color	지금하고 같은 색으로 좀 해 주세요 *jigeumhago gateun saegeuro jom hae juseyo*
I'd like it darker/lighter ____	더 어둡게/ 밝게 좀 해 주세요 *deo eodupge/balkke jom hae juseyo*
I'd like/I don't want ____ hairspray	헤어 스프레이 해 주세요./하지 마세요 *heeo seupeurei hae juseyo./haji maseyo*
gel ____	젤 *jel*

lotion	로션
	rosyeon
I'd like short bangs _____	앞머리 짧게 좀 해 주세요
	ammeori jjalkke jom hae juseyo
Not too short at the back __	뒤는 너무 짧지 않게 해 주세요
	dwineun neomu jjaljji anke hae juseyo
Not too long. _____	너무 길지 않게 해 주세요
	neomu gilji anke hae juseyo
I'd like it curly/not too _____ curly	곱슬곱슬하게/ 너무 곱슬곱슬하지 않게 좀 해 주세요.
	gopseulgopseulhage/neomu gopseulgopseulhaji anke jom hae juseyo
It needs a little/a lot taken__ off	약간/많이 좀 쳐 주세요
	yakgan/mani jom chyeo juseyo
I'd like a completely _____ different style/cut	완전히 다른 스타일로/ 컷트로 좀 해 주세요
	wanjeonhi dareun seutaillo/keoteuro jom hae juseyo
I'd like it the same as in____ this photo	이 사진처럼 좀 해 주세요
	i sajinchereom jom hae juseyo
as that woman's _____	저 여자처럼
	jeo yeojachreom
Could you turn the drier ___ up/down a bit?	드라이어 좀 올려/내려 주시겠어요?
	deuraieo jom ollyeo/naeryeo jusigesseoyo?
I'd like a facial_____	얼굴 손질 좀 해 주세요
	eolgul sonjil jom hae juseyo
a manicure _____	손톱 손질
	sontop sonjil
a massage_____	마사지
	masaji
Could you trim my..., _____ please?	제 ... 좀 다듬어 주시겠어요?
	je ... jom dadeumeo jusigesseoyo?
bangs _____	앞머리
	ammeori
beard_____	턱수염
	teoksuyeom
moustache_____	콧수염
	kotsuyeom
I'd like a shave, please____	면도 좀 해주세요
	myeondo jom hae juseyo

Shopping

10

어떻게 잘라 드릴까요?	How do you want it cut?
무슨 스타일을 원하세요?	What style did you have in mind?
무슨 칼라를 원하세요?	What color did you want it?
온도가 괜찮으세요?	Is the temperature all right for you?
읽을 거 드릴까요?	Would you like something to read?
마실 거 드릴까요?	Would you like a drink?
이게 원하시던 거예요?	Is this what you had in mind?

At the Tourist Information Center

At the Tourist Information Center

● **Tourist information and assistance** can easily be obtained from the Tourist Information Center (TIC) of the Korea National Tourism Organization (KNTO) in Seoul. The office is open every day from 9 a.m. to 9 p.m. and its phone number is (02) 757 0086. Tourist information is also available from the Seoul City Tourist Information Centers at major tourist attractions in Seoul, or from the information counters at the three international airports (Incheon, Gimhae, and Jeju), or from major transportation terminals such as railway stations and ferry or bus terminals in major cities. There is also the Korea Travel Phone service offering tourist information and assistance in English. Just call 1330 to get detailed travel information about most areas in the country.

11 .1 Places of interest

Where's the Tourist_____ Information, please?	관광 안내소가 어디에 있어요? *gwan-gwang annaesoga eodie isseoyo?*
Do you have a city map?___	시내 지도 있어요? *sinae jido isseoyo?*
Where is the museum? ___	박물관이 어디에 있어요? *bangmulgwani eodie isseoyo?*
Where can I find a_____ church?	교회가 어디에 있어요? *gyohoega eodie isseoyo?*
Could you give me some __ information about ...?	...에 대해서 안내 좀 해 주시겠어요? *...e daehaeseo annae jom hae jusigesseoyo?*
How much is this?_____	이거 얼마예요? *igeo eolmayeyo?*
What are the main places __ of interest?	관광명소가 어디예요? *gwan-gwangmyeongsoga eodiyeyo?*
Could you point them out__ on the map?	지도에서 어딘지 표시해 주시겠어요? *Jidoeseo eodinji pyosi hae jusigesseoyo?*
What do you_____ recommend?	어디를 추천하시겠어요? *eodireul chucheonhasigesseoyo?*
We'll be here for a few hours	여기 두 세 시간 있을 거예요 *yeogi du se sigan isseul geoyeyo*
We'll be here for a day ___	여기 하루 있을 거예요 *yeogi haru isseul geoyeyo*
We'll be here for a week ___	여기 일 주일 있을 거예요 *yeogi il juil isseul geoyeyo*
We're interested in... _____	...에 관심이 있어요 *...e gwansimi isseoyo*
Is there a scenic walk_____ around the city?	시내 근처에 전망이 좋은 산책로 있어요? *sinae geuncheo-e jeonmang-i jo-eun sanchaengno isseoyo?*
How long does it take? ____	얼마나 걸려요? *eolmana geollyeoyo?*
Where does it start/end? ___	어디에서 시작돼요?/끝나요? *eodieseo sijakdwaeyo?/kkeunnayo?*
Are there any boat trips? __	유람선 투어 있어요? *yuramseon tueo isseoyo?*
Where can we board? _____	어디에서 타요? *eodieseo tayo?*
Are there any bus tours?___	관광버스 투어가 있어요? *gwan.gwangbeoseu tueoga isseoyo?*

Where do we get on?	어디에서 타요? *eodieseo tayo?*
Is there a guide who speaks English?	영어 할 줄 아는 가이드 있어요? *yeong-eohal jul aneun gaideu isseoyo?*
What trips can we take around the area?	그 지역에 어떤 투어가 있어요? *geu jiyeoge eotteon tueoga isseoyo?*
Are there any excursions?	야외 투어가 있어요? *ya-oe tueoga isseoyo?*
Where do they go?	어디 어디로 가요? *eodi eodiro gayo?*
We'd like to go to ...	...에 가고 싶어요 *...e jom gago sipeoyo*
How long is the excursion?	그 투어는 얼마나 걸려요? *geu tueoneun eolmana geolyeoyo?*
How long do we stay in ...?	...에 얼마나 오래 있어요? *...eolmana orae isseoyo?*
Are there any guided tours?	가이드 투어가 있어요? *gaideu tueoga isseoyo?*
How much free time will we have there?	거기에서 자유시간이 얼마나 있어요? *geogieseo jayusigani eolmana isseoyo?*
We want to have a walk around/to go on foot	걸어서 다니고 싶어요 *georeoseo dora danigo sipeoyo*
Can we hire a guide?	가이드를 고용할 수 있어요? *gaideureul goyonghal su isseoyo?*
What time does ... open/close?	몇 시에 ...열어요/닫아요? *myeot sie ...yeoreoyo/dadayo?*
What days is ... open/closed?	무슨 요일에 ...열어요/닫아요? *museun yoire ...yeoreoyo/dadayo?*
What's the admission price?	입장가 얼마예요? *ipjangnyoga eolmayeyo?*
Is there a group discount?	단체 할인 돼요? *danche harin dwaeyo?*
Is there a child discount?	어린이 할인 돼요? *eorini harin dwaeyo?*
Is there a discount for senior citizens?	경노 할인 돼요? *gyeongno harin dwaeyo?*
Can I take (flash) photos here?	(플래쉬) 사진 찍어도 돼요? *(peullaeswi) sajin jjigeodo dwaeyo?*
Do you have any postcards of ...?	...엽서 있어요? *...yeopseo isseoyo?*
Do you have an English ...?	영어 ...있어요? *yeong.eo ...isseoyo?*
catalog	카타로그 *katarogeu*
program	프로그램 *peurogeuraem*
brochure	브로슈어 *beurosyueo*

11 .2 Going out

Do you have this week's/month's entertainment guide?	이번 주/달 공연 안내서 있어요? *ibeon ju/dal gong-yeon annaeseo isseoyo?*
What's on tonight?	오늘 저녁에 뭐 해요? *oneul jeonyeoge mwo haeyo?*
We want to go to...	...에 가고 싶어요 *...e gago sipeoyo*
What's on at the cinema?	극장에서 뭐 해요? *geukjang-eseo mwo haeyo?*
What sort of film is that?	어떤 영화예요? *eotteon yeonghwayeyo?*
suitable for everyone	누구나 볼 수 있는 *nuguna bol su inneun*
not suitable for people under 18	열여덟 살 이하는 볼 수 없는 *yeolyeodeop sal iha-neun bol su eopneun*
original version	오리지날 판 *orijinal pan*
subtitled	자막이 나오는 *jamagi naoneun*
dubbed	더빙이 된 *deobing-i doen*
Is it a continuous showing?	연속상영이에요? *yeonsok sangyeong.ieyo?*
What's on at...?	...에서는 뭐 해요? *...enseo-neuun mwo haeyo?*
the theater	극장 *geukjang*
the opera	오페라 극장 *opera geukjang*
What's happening in the concert hall?	콘서트 홀에서는 뭐 해요? *konseoteu horeseoneun mwo haeyo?*
Where can I find a good night club around here?	이 근처에서 좋은 나이트 클럽이 어디에 있어요? *i geuncheo-eseo jo-eun naiteu keulleopi eodie isseoyo?*
Is it members only?	회원 전용이에요? *hoewon jeonyong-ieyo?*
Is it evening wear only?	야회복을 꼭 입어야 돼요? *yahoebogeul kkok ibeoya dwaeyo?*
Should I/we dress up?	정장을 입어야 돼요? *jeongjangeul ibeoya dwaeyo?*
What time does the show start?	몇 시에 공연이 시작돼요? *myeot sie gongyeoni sijakdwaeyo?*
When's the next soccer match?	다음 축구경기가 언제 있어요? *da-eum chugugyeongga eonje isseoyo?*
I'd like an escort for tonight	오늘 저녁에 파트너가 필요해요 *oneul jeonyeoge pateuneoga piryohaeyo*

11 .3 Reserving tickets

At the Tourist Information Center

Could you reserve some ___ tickets for us?	티켓을 몇 장 예약해 주시겠어요? *tiketeul myeot jang yeyakhae jusigesseoyo?*
We'd like to book... _____ seats/a table for...	좌석 ...개/...인용 테이블 하나를 예약하고 싶어요. *jwaseok ...gae/...inyong teibeul hanareul yeyakhago sipeoyo*
...seats in the orchestra ___ in the main section	오케스트라석 ...장 *okeseuteuraseok ...jang*
...seats in the circle _____	이층석 ...장 *yicheungseok ...jang*
a box for... _____	...인용 박스석 하나 *...inyong bakseuseok hana*
...front row seats/a table ___ for...at the front	앞줄 좌석 ...장 /...인용 앞쪽 테이블 하나 *apjul jwaseok ...jang/...inyong apjjok teibeul hana*
...seats in the middle/a _____ table in the middle	중간 좌석 ...장/ 중간 테이블 하나 *junggan jwaseok ...jang/junggan teibeul hana*
...back row seats/a table ___ at the back	뒷줄 좌석 ...장/뒤쪽 테이블 하나 *dwitjul jwaseok ...jang/dwijjok teibeul hana*
Could I reserve...seats _____ for the...o'clock performance?	...시 공연 좌석 ....장 예약해 주시겠어요? *...si gong-yeon jwaseok ...jang yeyakhae jusigesseoyo?*
Are there any seats left ____ for tonight?	오늘 저녁 좌석 남은 거 있어요? *oneul jeonyeok jwaseok nameun geo isseoyo?*
How much is a ticket? _____	티켓 한 장에 얼마예요? *tiket han jang.e eolmayeyo?*
When can I pick up the ____ tickets?	언제 티켓 찾으러 갈까요? *eonje tiket chajeureo galkkayo?*
I've got a reservation _____	예약했어요 *yeyakhaesseoyo*
My name is... _____	제 이름은 ...이에요 *je ireumeun ...ieyo*

11

어느 공연을 예약하시고 싶으세요? _____	Which performance do you want to reserve for?
어디에 앉으시고 싶으세요? _____	Where would you like to sit?
전부 매진입니다 _____	Everything's sold out
입석만 있습니다 _____	It's standing room only
이층석만 남았습니다 _____	We've only got circle seats left
삼층석만 남았습니다 _____	We've only got upper circle (way upstairs) seats left
오케스트라석만 남았습니다 _____	We've only got orchestra seats left
앞줄 좌석만 남았습니다 _____	We've only got front row seats left

뒷줄 좌석만 남았습니다_____	We've only got seats left at the back
좌석 몇 개가 필요하세요? _____	How many seats would you like?
...시 이전에 티켓을 찾아 가셔야 합니다 ___	You'll have to pick up the tickets before...o'clock
티켓, 부탁합니다_____	Tickets, please
여기가 손님 좌석입니다_____	This is your seat
좌석을 잘못 앉으셨어요_____	You are in the wrong seat

At the Tourist Information Center

11

12 Sports

12 Sports

● **Many beaches, lakes and rivers** including the Han River in Seoul offer a wide range of summer sports such as water skiing, canoeing, scuba diving, wind surfing and rafting. There are also several world-class ski resorts that are open from mid December until early March. During the season, major travel agencies operate bus trips between Seoul and the resorts. The most popular spectator sports are baseball and soccer.

12 .1 Sporting questions

Where can we ... around here?	이 근처 어디에서 ...(으)ㄹ 수 있어요? *i geuncheo eodieseo -(eu)l su isseoyo?*
Can we hire a ...?	...빌릴 수 있어요? *...billil su isseoyo?*
Can we take ... lessons?	...강습 받을 수 있어요? *...gangseup badeul su isseoyo?*
How much is that per hour/per day?	시간에/하루에 얼마예요? *sigane/harue eolmayeyo?*
How much is each one?	각 각 얼마예요? *gak gak eolmayeyo?*
Do you need a permit for that?	허가를 받아야 돼요? *heogareul badaya dwaeyo?*
Where can I get the permit?	어디에서 허가를 받을 수 있어요? *eodieseo heogareul badeul su isseoyo?*

12 .2 By the waterfront

Is it far (to walk) to the sea?	바다까지 (걷기에) 멀어요? *badakkaji (geotgie) meoreoyo?*
Is there a...around here?	이 근처에 ...있어요? *i geuncheo-e ...isseoyo?*
a swimming pool	수영장 *suyeongjang*
a sandy beach	모래 사장 *morae sajang*
mooring place	선착장 *seonchakjang*
Are there any sunken rocks here?	여기 암초가 있어요? *yeogi amchoga isseoyo?*
When is high/low tide?	썰물이/밀물이 언제예요? *sseolmuri/milmuri eonjeyeyo?*
What's the water temperature?	수온은 어떻게 돼요? *suoneun eotteoke dwaeyo?*
Is it (very) deep here?	여기 (아주) 깊어요? *yeogi (aju) gipeoyo?*
Is it safe (for children) to swim here?	여기 (어린이가) 수영하기가 안전해요? *yeogi (eoringa) suyeonghagiga anjeonhaeyo?*
Are there any currents?	물살이 강한 곳이 있어요? *Mulsari gang-han gosi isseoyo?*
Are there any rapids/ waterfalls along this river?	이 강에 급류가/ 폭포가 있어요? *i gang-e geumnyuga/pokpoga isseoyo?*
What does that flag/buoy mean?	저 깃발이/부표가 무슨 뜻이에요? *jeo gitbari/bupyoga museun tteusieyo?*

Is there a lifeguard on duty?	인명 구조원이 있어요?
	inmyeong gujowoni isseoyo?
Are dogs allowed here?	여기 개를 데리고 와도 돼요?
	yeogi gaereul derigo wado dwaeyo?
Is camping on the beach allowed?	바닷가에서 캠핑해도 돼요?
	badatga-eseo kaemping.haedo dwaeyo?
Can we light a fire?	불을 피워도 돼요?
	bureul piwodo dwaeyo?

낚시터	서핑금지	수영금지
Fishing waters	No surfing	No swimming
면허소지자에 한함	위험	낚시금지
Permits only	Danger	No fishing

.3 In the snow

Can I take ski lessons here?	여기에서 스키강습 받을 수 있어요?
	yegieseo seuki gangseup badeul su isseoyo?
For beginners/ intermediates/ advanced	초급/중급/고급
	chogeup/junggeup/gogeup
How large are the groups?	반이 얼마나 커요?
	bani eolmana keoyo?
What languages are the classes in?	강습에서 어떤 언어를 써요?
	gangseubeseo eotteon eoneoreul sseoyo?
I'd like a lift pass, please	리프트 패스 하나 주세요
	ripeuteu paeseu hana juseyo
Where are the beginner's slopes?	초급 코스는 어디에 있어요?
	chogeup koseuneun eodie isseoyo?
Are there any cross-country ski runs around here?	크로스 칸츄리 코스가 있어요?
	keuroseu kanchyuri koseuga isseoyo?
Have the cross-country runs been marked?	크로스 칸츄리 코스에 표시가 있어요?
	keuroseu kanchyuri koseue pyosiga isseoyo?
Are the ... open?	...열었어요?
	...yeoreotseoyo?
the ski lifts	스키 리프트
	seuki ripeuteu
the chair lifts	리프트
	ripeuteu
the runs	코스
	koseu
the cross-country runs	크로스 칸츄리 코스
	keuroseu kanchyuri koseu

Sports

12

Sickness

13 Sickness

● **You can see** any specialist or doctor without having a GP's referral. Most doctors in hospitals in Korea speak some basic English. However, if you are in Seoul, it is recommended that you see the doctors in the International Clinics of general hospitals such as the Severance Hospital, Asan Medical Centre, or Samsung Medical Centre. You can buy medication for common illnesses over the counter at pharmacists without a doctor's prescription.

13.1 Call (get) the doctor

Could you call a doctor quickly, please?	의사 좀 빨리 불러 주시겠어요? *uisa jom ppalli bulleo jusigesseoyo?*
When is the doctor in?	진료시간이 어떻게 돼요? *jillyosigani eotteoke dwaeyo?*
When can the doctor come?	언제 의사가 올 수 있어요? *eonje uisaga ol su isseoyo?*
Could I make an appointment to see the doctor?	진료예약을 할 수 있을까요? *jillyoyeyageul hal su isseulkkayo?*
I've got an appointment to see the doctor at ...o'clock	...시에 진료예약을 했어요 *...sie jillyo yeyageul haesseoyo*
Which doctor/pharmacy is on night/weekend duty	어느 의사가/약국이 밤에/주말에 일해요? *eoneu uisaga/yakgugi bame/jumare ilhaeyo?*

13.2 Patient's ailments

I don't feel well	몸이 안 좋아요 *momi an joayo*
I'm dizzy	어지러워요 *eojireowoyo*
I'm sick.	아파요 *apayo*
I feel nauseous	메스꺼워요 *meskkeowoyo*
I've got a cold	감기에 걸렸어요 *gamgie geollyeosseoy*
It hurts here	여기가 아파요 *yeogiga apayo*
I vomited	토했어요 *tohaesseoyo*
I've got ...	...이/가 있어요 *...i/ga isseoyo*
I'm running a temperature of ...degrees	체온이 ...도나 돼요. *choni ...dona dwaeyo*
I've been stung by ...	...에 쏘였어요 *...e ssoyeosseoyo*
a wasp	벌 *beol*
an insect	벌레 *beolle*
a jellyfish	해파리 *haepari*

I've been bitten by... _____	...에 물렸어요
	...e mullyeosseoyo
a dog _____	개
	gae
a snake _____	뱀
	baem
an animal _____	동물
	dongmul
I've cut myself _____	상처를 냈어요
	sangcheoreul naesseoyo
I've burned myself _____	화상을 입었어요
	hwasang-eul ibeosseoyo
I've grazed myself _____	찰과상을 입었어요
	chalgwasang-eul ibeosseoyo
I've had a fall _____	넘어졌어요
	neomeojyeosseoyo
I've sprained my ankle _____	발목을 삐었어요
	balmogeul ppieosseoyo

.3 The consultation

어떤 문제인 것 같아요? _____	What seems to be the problem?
이런 증세가 얼마나 오래됐어요? _____	How long have you had these complaints?
전에 이런 문제가 있었어요? _____	Have you had this trouble before?
열이 있어요? 얼마나 높아요? _____	Do you have a temperature? What is it?
옷을 벗으세요 _____	Get undressed, please
허리까지 벗으세요 _____	Strip to the waist, please
저기에서 벗으시면 돼요 _____	You can undress there
왼쪽/오른쪽 소매를 걷어 올려 주세요 ____	Roll up your left/right sleeve, please
여기에 누우세요 _____	Lie down here, please
이렇게 하면 아파요? _____	Does this hurt?
숨을 깊이 쉬세요 _____	Breathe deeply
입을 벌리세요 _____	Open your mouth

Patients' medical history

I'm a diabetic _____	당뇨병이 있어요
	dannyobyeong-i isseoyo
I have a heart condition ____	심장질환이 있어요
	simjangjilhwani isseoyo
I'm asthmatic _____	천식이 있어요
	cjeonsigi isseoyo
I'm allergic to ... _____	...에 알레르기가 있어요
	...allereugiga isseoyo
I'm ...months pregnant ____	임신 ...개월이에요
	imsin ...gaeworieyo
I'm on a diet _____	지금 식이요법을 하고 있어요
	jigeum sigiyoppeobeul hago isseoyo

Sickness

13

I'm on medication	지금 약을 먹고 있어요
	jigeum yageul meokgo isseoyo
I've had a heart attack once before	전에 한번 심장마비를 한 적이 있어요
	jeone hanbeon simjangmabiga on jeogi isseoyo
I've had a(n) ...operation	...수술을 한 적이 있어요
	...susureul han jeogi isseoyo
I've been ill recently	최근에 아팠어요
	choegeune apasseoyo
I've got a stomach ulcer	위궤양이 있어요
	wigweyang-i isseoyo
I've got my period	생리 중이에요
	saeng-ni jung.ieyo

알레르기가 있어요?	Do you have any allergies?
지금 약을 복용 중이신가요?	Are you on any medication?
지금 식이요법 중 이신가요?	Are you on a diet?
임신 중이신가요?	Are you pregnant?
파상풍 주사를 맞으신 적이 있나요?	Have you had a tetanus injection?

The diagnosis

심각한 건 아니에요	It's nothing serious
...이/가 부러졌네요	Your ...is broken
...삐었군요.	You've got a sprained ...
...이/가 찢어졌군요	You've got a torn ...
염증이 있군요	You've got some inflammation
맹장염이군요	You've got appendicitis
기관지염이군요	You've got bronchitis
성병이군요	You've got a venereal disease
독감이군요	You've got the flu
심장마비이군요	You've had a heart attack
(바이러스성/ 박테리아성) 염증이에요	You've got a (viral/bacterial) infection
폐렴이에요	You've got pneumonia
위염/위궤양이에요	You've got gastritis/an ulcer
근육이 늘어났군요	You've pulled a muscle
질염이군요	You've got a vaginal infection
식중독이에요	You've got food poisoning
일사병이에요	You've got sunstroke
...에 알레르기가 있군요	You're allergic to ...
임신이군요	You're pregnant
피/ 소변/대변 검사를 해야겠어요	I'd like to have your blood/urine/stools tested
봉합 수술이 필요해요	It needs stitches

Sickness

13

전문의한테 보내드리겠어요	I'm referring you to a specialist
엑스레이를 찍어야겠어요	You'll need some x-rays taken
대기실에서 좀 기다려 주시겠어요?	Could you wait in the waiting room, please?
수술을 해야겠어요	You'll need an operation

Is it contagious?	이거 전염돼요? *igeo jeonyeomdwaeyo?*
How long do I have to stay ...?	얼마나 오래 ...있어야 돼요? *eolmana orae ...isseoya dwaeyo?*
in bed	누워 *nuwo*
in the hospital	병원에 *byeong-wone*
Do I have to go on a special diet?	식이요법을 해야 돼요? *sigiyobeobeul haeya dwaeyo?*
Am I allowed to travel?	여행을 해도 돼요? *yeohaeng-eul haedo dwaeyo?*
Can I make another appointment?	다음 예약 할 수 있어요? *Daeum yeyageul hal su isseoyo?*
When do I have to come back?	언제 다시 와야 돼요? *eonje dasi waya dwaeyo?*
I'll come back tomorrow	내일 다시 오겠어요 *naeil dasi ogesseoyo*
How do I take this medicine?	이 약 어떻게 먹어요? *i yak eotteoke meogeoyo?*

내일/...일 후에 다시 오세요	Come back tomorrow/in ...days' time

13 .4 Medication and prescriptions

How many pills/drops/spoonfuls/tablets each time?	한 번에 몇 알/방울/ 스푼/알씩이에요? *han beone myeot al/bang-ul/seupun/alssigieyo?*
How many times a day?	하루에 몇 번씩이요? *harue myeot beonssigiyo?*
I've forgotten my medication	약 먹는 것을 잊어버렸어요 *yak meongneun geoseul ijeobeoryeosseoyo*
Could you write a prescription for me, please?	처방전 좀 써 주시겠어요? *cheobangjeon jom sseo jusigesseoyo?*

항생제/감기 물약/ 진정제/진통제 처방 ____ 해드릴께요	I'm prescribing antibiotics/ a cough mixture/a tranquilizer/pain killers
푹 쉬세요 ____	Have lots of rest
집에 계세요 ____	Stay indoors
누워 계세요 ____	Stay in bed

캡슐 capsules	물에 녹이세요 dissolve in water	이 약은 운전에 장애 를 가져옵니다 This medication impairs your driving
알약 pills/tablets	고루 바르세요 rub on	
점적약 drops	한 숟갈/한 찻숟갈 spoonful/teaspoonful	처방전의 약을 끝까지 드세요 Finish the prescription
주사 injections	식전에 before meals	
연고 ointment	매 ...시간마다 every ...hours	외용 External use only
드세요 take	하루에 ... 번 씩 ...times a day	
(통째로) 삼키세요 swallow (whole)	... 일 동안 for ...days	

13 .5 At the dentist's

Do you know a good dentist?	잘 하는 치과 의사 아세요? jal haneun chikkwa uisa aseyo?
Could you make a dentists appointment for me?	치과에 예약 좀 해 주시겠어요? chikkwa-e yeyak jom hae jusigesseoyo?
It's urgent	급해요 geupaeyo
Can I come in today, please?	오늘 가도 돼요? oneul gado dwaeyo?
I have a (terrible) toothache	이가 (심하게) 아파요 iga (simhage) apayo
Could you prescribe/give me a painkiller?	진통제 좀 처방해 주시겠어요? jitongje jom cheobang hae jusigesseoyo?
I've got a broken tooth	이가 부러졌어요 iga bureojyeosseoyo
My filling's come out	이 떼운 게 빠졌어요 i ttaeun ge ppajyeosseoyo
I've got a broken crown	이 씌운 게 망가졌어요 i sswiun ge mang-gajyeosseoyo
I'd like/I don't want a local anaesthetic	국부 마취를 해 주세요/ 하지 마세요 gukbu machwireul hae juseyo/haji maseyo
Could you do a temporary repair?	임시처방을 좀 해주시겠어요? Imsicheobang-eul jom haejusigesseoyo?
I don't want this tooth pulled	이 이를 빼고 싶지 않아요 i ireul ppaego sipji anayo
My denture is broken	틀니가 망가졌어요 teulliga mang-gajyeosseoyo
Can you fix it?	고칠 수 있어요? gochil su isseoyo?

Sickness

13

어느 이가 아프세요?	Which tooth hurts?
고름이 생겼어요	You've got an abscess
근관치료를 해야겠어요	I'll have to do a root canal
국부 마취를 해야겠어요	I'm giving you a local anaesthetic
이 이를 뽑아야/때워야/갈아야 되겠어요	I'll have to pull/fill/file this tooth
드릴을 해야겠어요	I'll have to drill it
입을 크게 벌리세요	Open wide, please
입을 다무세요	Close your mouth, please
입을 헹구세요	Rinse, please
아직도 아프세요?	Does it hurt still?

In trouble

14 In trouble

● **In an emergency,** call 112 for the police and 119 for the fire or ambulance service. Many police boxes are located on the major streets of most cities. Alternatively, you can call the International SOS Korea (Tel: 02 790 7561) for 24-hour emergency service assistance in English. For lost property, contact the Lost and Found Center of the Seoul Metropolitan Police Bureau (Tel: 02 2299 1282).

14 .1 Asking for help

Help! — 도와 주세요!
dowa juseyo!

Fire! — 불이 났어요!
buri nasseoyo!

Police! — 경찰요!
gyeongcharyo!

Quick/Hurry! — 빨리요!
ppalliyo!

Danger! — 위험해요!
wiheomhaeyo!

Watch out! — 조심하세요!
josimhaseyo!

Stop! — 멈추세요!
meomchseyo!

Be careful!/Go easy! — 조심하세요!
josimhaseyo!

Get your hands off me! — 손 치워요!
son chiwoyo!

Stop thief! — 도둑이야!
dodugiya!

Could you help me, please? — 저 좀 도와 주시겠어요?
jeo jom dowa jusigesseoyo?

Where's the police station/emergency exit/fire escape? — 경찰서/비상구/비상구가 어디에 있어요?
gyeongchalseo/bisang-gu/bisang-guga eodie isseoyo?

Where's the nearest fire extinguisher? — 소화기가 어디에 있어요?
sohwagiga eodie isseoyo?

Call the fire department! — 소방서에 연락하세요!
Sobangseo-e yeollakhaseyo!

Call the police! — 경찰에 연락하세요!
gyeongchale yeollakhaseyo!

Call an ambulance! — 앰뷸런스를 부르세요!
ambyulleonseureul bureuseyo!

Where's the nearest phone? — 전화가 어디에 있어요?
jenhwaga eodie isseoyo?

Could I use your phone? — 전화 좀 써도 돼요?
jeonhwa jom sseodo dwaeyo?

What's the emergency number? — 응급 전화가 몇 번이에요?
eunggeup jeonhwaga myeot neonieyo?

What's the number for the police? — 경찰 전화가 몇 번이에요?
gyeongchal jeonhwaga myeot neonieyo?

I've lost my wallet/purse — 지갑을 잃어버렸어요
jigabeul ireobeoryeosseoyo

14 .2 Loss

I lost my ...here yesterday	어제 여기서 ...을/를 잃어버렸어요
	eoje yeogiseo ...eul/reul ireobeoryeosseoyo
I left my ...here	여기에 ...을/를 두었어요
	yeogie ...eul/reul dueosseoyo
Did you find my...?	제 ... 찾았어요?
	je ... chajasseoyo?
It was right here	바로 여기에 있었어요
	baro yeogie isseosseoyo
It's very valuable	아주 소중한 거예요
	aju sojung-han geoyeyo
Where's the lost and found office?	분실물센터가 어디에 있어요?
	bunsilmulsenteoga eodie isseoyo?

14 .3 Accidents

There's been an accident	사고가 났어요
	sagoga nasseoyo.
Someone's fallen into the water	누가 물에 빠졌어요
	nuga mure ppajyeosseoyo
There's a fire	불이 났어요
	buri nasseoyo
Is anyone hurt?	다친 사람 있어요?
	dachin saram isseoyo?
Nobody has been injured	아무도 안 다쳤어요
	amudo an dachyeosseoyo
Someone has been injured	누가 다쳤어요
	nuga dachyeosseoyo
Someone's still trapped inside the car/train	누가 아직도 차/기차 안에 갇혀 있어요
	nuga ajikdo cha/gicha ane gatchyeo isseoyo
It's not too bad	아주 나쁘진 않아요
	aju nappeujin anayo
Don't worry	걱정하지 마세요
	geokjeonghaji maseyo
Leave everything the way it is, please	있는 그대로 두세요
	inneun geudaero duseyo
I want to talk to the police first	먼저 경찰에 신고해야겠어요
	meonjeo gyeongchare sin.gohaeyagesseoyo
I want to take a photo first	먼저 사진을 찍어야겠어요
	meonjeo sajineul jjigeoyagesseoyo
Here's my name and address	여기 제 이름과 주소가 있어요
	yeogi je ireumgwa jusoga isseoyo
May I have your name and address?	성함과 주소 좀 주시겠어요?
	Seong-hamgwa juso jom jusigesseoyo?
Could I see your identity card/your insurance papers?	신분증/보험증 좀 보여 주시겠어요?
	sinbunjjeung/boheomjjeung jom boyeo jusigesseoyo?
Would you act as a witness?	증인이 좀 돼 주시겠어요?
	Jeung-ini jom dwae jusigesseoyo?
I need this information for insurance purposes	보험 청구에 이 내용이 필요해요
	Boheom cheong-gue i naeyoung.i piryohaeyo
Are you insured?	보험 들었어요?
	boheom deureosseoyo?

In trouble

14

Third party or all inclusive?	삼자 대물 보험 아니면 종합 보험이에요?
	samja daemul boheom animyeon jonghap boheomieyo?
Could you sign here, please?	여기 사인 좀 해 주시겠어요?
	yeogi sain jom hae jusigesseoyo?

14.4 Theft

I've been robbed	도둑맞았어요
	doduk majasseoyo
My ...has been stolen	...을/를 도둑맞았어요
	...eul/reul doduk majasseoyo
My car's been broken into	제 차에 도둑이 들었어요
	je cha-e dodugi deureosseoyo

14.5 Missing person

I've lost my child/ grandmother	우리 애/할머니가 없어졌어요
	uri ae/halmeoniga eopseojyeosseoyo
Could you help me find him/her?	좀 찾아주시겠어요?
	jom chaja jusigesseoyo?
Have you seen a small child?	어린 아이를 못 보셨나요?
	eorin aireul mot bosyeossnayo?
He's/She's ...years old	나이는 ...살이에요
	naineun ...sarieyo
He/She's got ...hair	...머리예요
	...meoriyeyo
short/long	짧은/ 긴
	jjalbeun/gin
blond/red/brown/ black/grey	금발/ 빨간색/갈색/ 검은색/ 회색
	geumbal/ppalgansaek/galsaek/geomeunsaek/ hoesaek
curly/straight/frizzy	웨이브가 있는/ 일자/ 곱슬곱슬한
	weibeuga inneun/ ilja/ gopseulgopseulhan
in a ponytail	뒤로 묶은
	dwiro mukkeon
in braids	땋은
	ttaeun
in a bun	뒤로 올린
	dwiro ollin
He's/She's got blue/ brown/green eyes	눈은 파란색/ 갈색/푸른색 눈이에요
	nuneun paransaek/galsek/pureunsaek nunieyo
He's/She's wearing swimming trunks	반바지 수영복을 입고 있어요
	banbaji suyeongbogeul ipgo isseoyo
He's/She's wearing hiking boots	등산화를 신고 있어요
	deungsanhwareul sinkko isseoyo
with/without glasses	안경을 끼고/ 안 끼고
	angyeong-eul kkigo/an kkigo
carrying/not carrying a bag	가방을 들고/ 안 들고
	gabang-eul deulgo/an deulgo
He/She is tall/short	키가 커요/작아요
	kiga keoyo/jagayo
This is a photo of him/her	이게 그 애 사진이에요
	ige geu ae sajinieyo
He/she must be lost	틀림없이 길을 잃었어요
	teullimeopsi gireul ireosseoyo

14 .6 The police

An arrest

면허증 좀 보여 주세요	Your driver's license, please
속도위반입니다	You were speeding
여기 주차하시면 안 됩니다	You're not allowed to park here
주차비를 안 내셨습니다	You haven't put money in the parking meter
라이트가 안 들어옵니다	Your lights aren't working
... 원 벌금입니다	That's a ... won fine
지금 내시겠습니까?	Do you want to pay now?
지금 내셔야 합니다	You'll have to pay now

I don't speak Korean	한국말 못 합니다
	hanggungmal mot hamnida
I didn't see the sign	표지판을 못 봤어요
	pyojipaneul mot bwasseoyo
I don't understand what it says	무슨 말인지 모르겠어요
	museun marinji moreugeosseoyo
I was only doing ... kilometers an hour	시속 ... 키로였는데요
	danji ... kiroyeonneundeyo
I'll have my car checked	차 정비를 맡기겠어요
	cha jeongnireul matgigeosseoyo
I was blinded by oncoming lights	맞은편 차량 불빛 때문에 볼 수가 없었어요
	majeunpyeon charyang bulbit-ttaemune bol suga eopsseosseoyo

어디서 일어났습니까?	Where did it happen?
뭐가 없어졌습니까?	What's missing?
뭘 가져갔습니까?	What's been taken?
신분증 좀 보여 주시겠습니까?	Could I see your identity card/some identification?
그게 몇 시였습니까?	What time did it happen?
증인이 있습니까?	Are there any witnesses?
여기 서명하세요	Sign here, please
통역이 필요하십니까?	Do you want an interpreter?

At the police station

I want to report a collision/missing person/rape	추돌 사고를/실종사건을/강간사건을 신고하고싶어요
	Chungdol sagoreul/siljjong sakkeuneul/ganggan sakkeoneul sin.go hago sipeoyo
Could you make a statement, please?	진술서를 좀 써 주시겠어요?
	jinsulseoreul jom sseo jusigesseoyo?

In trouble

14

106

Could I have a copy for the insurance?	보험용으로 사본 한 장 좀 주시겠어요? *Boheomyong-euro sabon han jang jom jusigesseoyo?*
I've lost everything _____	다 잃어버렸어요 *da ireobeoryeosseoyo*
I've no money left _____	돈이 하나도 없어요 *doni hanado eopseoyo*
Could you lend me a little money?	돈을 조금 빌려 주시겠어요? *doneul jogeum billyeo jusigesseoyo?*
I'd like an interpreter _____	통역이 필요해요 *tongyeogi piryohaeyo*
I'm innocent _____	저는 죄가 없어요 *jeneun joega eopseoyo*
I don't know anything about it	그에 대해서 아무것도 모릅니다 *geue daehaeseo amugeotdo moreumnida*
I want to speak to someone from the ... embassy	... 대사관 직원과 얘기하고 싶어요 ... *daesagwan jigwon-gwa yaegihago sipeoyo*
I want a lawyer who speaks English	영어를 하는 변호사를 불러주세요 *Yeong-eoreul haneun byeonhosareul bulleo juseyo*

Word list

15

Word list English - Korean

● **This word list** is meant to supplement the previous chapters.
Some of the words not on this list can be found elsewhere in this book.
Food items can be found in Section 4.7, the parts of the car on pages
46-47, the parts of a motorcycle/bicycle on pages 50-51 and
camping/backpacking equipment on pages 64-65.

A

English	Korean	Romanization
about, approximately	...정도	...jeongdo
about, regarding	...에 대해	...e daehae
above, upstairs	...위에	...wie
abroad	해외에(서)	hae-oe-e(seo)
accident	사고	sago
adaptor	어댑터	eodaepteo
address	주소	juso
admission	입장	ipjang
admission price	입장료	ipjangnyo
adult	어른	eoreun
advice	충고	chunggo
aeroplane	비행기	bihaenggi
after	(place) 뒤에,	...dwie
	(time) 후에	...hue
afternoon	오후	ohu
aftershave	애프터 쉐이브	aepeuteo sweibeu
again	다시	dasi
age	나이	nai
AIDS	에이즈	eijeu
air conditioning	냉난방	naengnanbang
air mattress	공기 매트리스	gonggi maeteuriseu
airmail	항공 우편	hanggong upyeon
airplane	비행기	bihaenggi
airport	공항	gonghang
alarm (emergency)	경보	gyeongbo
alarm clock	알람 시계	allam sigye
alcohol, liquor	술	sul
all day	종일	jong-il
all the time	항상	hangsang
allergy	알레르기	allereugi
alone	혼자 있다, 혼자(서)	honjaitda, honja (seo)
altogether, in total	모두	modu
always	항상	hangsang
ambassador	대사	daesa
ambulance	앰뷸런스	aembyulleonseu
America	미국	miguk
American	미국 사람	miguk saram
amount	양, 금액	yang, geumaek
amusement park	놀이 공원	nori gong-won
anaesthetic (general)	전신 마취	jeonsin machwi
anaesthetic (local)	국부 마취	gukbu machwi
angry	화나다, 화난	hwanada, hwanan
animal	동물	dongmul
ankle	발목	balmok
answer the phone, to	전화 받다	jeonhwa batda

answer, respond (written), to	답장하다	*dapjanghada*
answer, respond, to	대답하다	*daedaphada*
answer, response (spoken)	대답	*daedap*
answer, response (written)	답장	*dapjang*
answering machine	자동 응답기	*jadong eungdapgi*
ant	개미	*gaemi*
antibiotics	항생제	*hangsaengje*
antifreeze	부동액	*budong-aek*
antiques	골동품	*golttongpum*
antiseptic	소독약	*sodong-yak*
anus	항문	*hangmun*
anybody, anyone	누구든지	*nugudeunji*
anything	무엇이든지	*mueosideunji*
anywhere	어디든지	*eodideunji*
apartment	아파트	*apateu*
apologise, to	사과하다	*sagwahada*
apple	사과	*sagwa*
apple juice	사과주스	*sagwajuseu*
apply (for permission), to	신청하다	*sincheonghada*
appointment	약속, 임명	*yaksok, immyeong*
April	사월	*sawol*
architecture	건축	*geonchuk*
area	지역	*jiyeok*
area code	지역 번호	*jiyeok beonho*
arm	팔	*pal*
arrange, to	준비하다	*junbihada*
arrival	도착	*dochak*
arrive, to	도착하다	*dochakhada*
arrow	화살	*hwasal*
art	예술	*yesul*
art gallery	미술관	*misulgwan*
artery	동맥	*dongmaek*
article (in newspaper)	기사	*gisa*
ashtray	재떨이	*jaetteori*
ask, to	물어보다	*mureoboda*
ask for, request, to	부탁하다	*butakhada*
aspirin	아스피린	*aseupirin*
assault	폭행	*pokhaeng*
assorted	종합한	*jonghaphan*
at home	집에	*jibe*
at night	밤에	*bame*
at the back	뒤에	*dwie*
at the front	앞에	*ape*
at the latest	늦어도	*neujeodo*
attractive	매력적이다/-적인	*maeryeokjeogida, maeryeokjeogin*
aubergine, eggplant	가지	*gaji*
August	팔월	*parwol*
Australia	호주	*hoju*
Australian	호주 사람	*hoju saram*
automatic	자동	*jadong*
autumn	가을	*ga-eul*
awake	깨어 있는	*kkae-eo ineun*
awning	차양	*chayang*

B

baby	아기	agi
baby food	이유식	iyusik
babysitter	보모	bomo
back (part of body)	등	deung
back, rear	뒤	dwi
backpack	배낭	baenang
backpacker	배낭 여행자	baenang yeohaengja
backward	뒤로	dwiro
bad (rotting)	상하다, 상한	sanghada, sanghan
bad (terrible)	나쁘다, 나쁜	nappeuda, nappeun
bag	가방	gabang
bakery	빵집	ppangjjip
balcony	발코니	balkoni
ball	공	gong
ball point pen	볼펜	bolpen
banana	바나나	banana
bandage	붕대	bungdae
bandaids	일회용 반창고	ilhoeyong banchanggo
bangs, fringe	앞머리	ammeori
bank (finance)	은행	eunhaeng
bank (river)	둑	duk
bar (caf)	카페	kape
barbecue	바베큐	babekyu
bargain, to	흥정하다	heungjeonghada
baseball	야구	yagu
basketball	농구	nonggu
bath	목욕	mogyok
bath towel	목욕 타월	mogyok tawol
bath mat	목욕탕 매트	mogyoktang maeteu
bathrobe	목욕 가운	mogyok gaun
bathroom	화장실, 목욕실	hwajangsil, mogyoksil
battery	밧데리	batderi
beach	바닷가	badatga
beans	콩	kong
beautiful (of people)	예쁘다, 예쁜	yeppeuda, yeppeun
beautiful (of places)	아름답다/-다운	areumdapda, areumdaun
beautiful (of things)	멋지다, 멋진	meotjida, meotjin
because	-기 때문에	-gi ttaemune
become, to	되다	doeda
bed	침대	chimdae
bedding, bedclothes	침구	chimgu
bee	벌	beol
beef	쇠고기	soegogi
beer	맥주	maekju
before (in front of)	앞에	ape
before (in time)	전에	jeone
begin, to	시작하다	sijakhada
behind	뒤에	dwie
below, downstairs	아래에	area-e
belt	벨트	belteu
berth	침대	chimdae
beside	옆에	yeope
better, get (improve), to	좋아지다	joajida
between	...사이에	...saie

bicycle	자전거	*jajeon-geo*
big	크다, 큰	*keuda, keun*
bikini	비키니	*bikini*
bill	계산서	*gyesanseo*
billiards	당구	*danggu*
birthday	생일	*saeng-il*
biscuit	비스켓, 과자	*biseuket, gwaja*
bite, to	물다	*mulda*
bitter	쓰다, 쓴	*sseuda, sseun*
black	까맣다, 까만	*kkamata, kkaman*
black and white	흑백	*heukbaek*
black eye	멍든 눈	*meongdeun nun*
bland (taste)	무미하다/- 한	*mumihada/-han*
blanket	담요	*damnyo*
bleach, to	탈색하다	*talsaekhada*
bleed, to	피를 흘리다	*pireul heullida*
blind (can't see)	눈이 멀다, 눈먼	*nuni meolda, nunmeon*
blind (on window)	블라인드	*beullaindeu*
blister	물집	*muljjip*
blond	금발	*geumbal*
blood	피	*pi*
blood pressure	혈압	*hyeorap*
bloody nose, to have	코피가 나다	*kopiga nada*
blouse	블라우스	*beullauseu*
blue	파랗다, 파란	*parata, paran*
boat	배	*bae*
body	몸	*mom*
boiled	끓인, 삶은	*kkeurin, salmeun*
bone	뼈	*ppyeo*
book	책	*chaek*
booked, reserved	예약되다, 예약된	*yeyakdoeda, yeyakdoen*
booking office	예매소	*yemaeso*
bookshop	서점	*seojeom*
border, edge	가장자리	*gajangjari*
bored	심심하다	*simsimhada*
boring	지루하다, 지루한	*jiruhada, jiruhan*
born, to be	태어나다	*tae-eonada*
borrow, to	빌리다	*billida*
botanic gardens	식물원	*singmurwon*
both	둘 다	*dul da*
bottle (baby's)	젖병	*jeotbyeong*
bottle (wine)	술병	*sulppyeong*
bottle-warmer	젖병 보온기	*jeotbyeong boon-gi*
box	상자	*sangja*
box office	매표소	*maepyoso*
boy	소년	*so-nyeon*
boyfriend	남자 친구	*namja chin-gu*
bra	브래지어	*beuraejieo*
bracelet	팔찌	*paljji*
brake	브레이크	*beureikeu*
brake oil	브레이크 오일	*beureikeu oil*
bread	빵	*ppang*
break, shatter, to	깨뜨리다	*kkaetteurida*
breakfast, morning meal	아침 식사	*achim siksa*
breast milk	모유	*moyu*

English	Korean	Romanization
breasts	가슴	gaseum
bridge	다리	dari
briefs	팬티	paenti
bring, to	가져오다	gajyeo-oda
brochure	브로셔	beurosyeo
broken (of bones, etc.)	부러지다, 부러진	bureojida, bureojin
broken, does not work	고장나다/-난	gojangnada, gojangnan
bronze	청동	cheongdong
broth, soup	국	guk
brother	형제	hyeongje
brown	갈색(의)	galsaek(ui)
bruise	멍	meong
brush	솔, 붓	sol, but
bucket	양동이	yangdong-i
Buddhism	불교	bulgyo
buffet	뷔페	bwipe
bugs	벌레	beolle
building	빌딩	bilding
bun	롤빵	rolppang
burglary	도난, 강도	donan, gangdo
burn (injury)	화상	hwasang
burn, to	태우다, 타다	tae-uda, tada
bus	버스	beoseu
bus station	버스 정거장	beoseu jeonggeojang
bus stop	버스 정류장	beoseu jeongnyujang
business card	명함	myeongham
business class	비지니스 클라스	bijinis keullas
business trip	출장	chuljang
busy (schedule)	바쁘다, 바쁜	bappeuda, bappeun
busy (traffic)	복잡하다, 복잡한	bokjaphada, bokjapan
but	그러나, -지만	geureona, -jiman
butane	부탄가스	butan gaseu
butchers	정육점	jeongyukjeom
butter	버터	beoteo
button	단추	danchu
buy, to	사다	sada
by airmail	항공우편으로	hanggong-upyeoneuro
by phone	전화로	jeonhwaro

C

English	Korean	Romanization
cabbage	양배추	yangbaechu
cabbage, Chinese	배추	baechu
cabin (boat)	선실	seonsil
cake, pastry	케이크	keikeu
call (phone call)	전화	jeonhwa
call, phone, to	전화하다	jeonhwahada
called, named	불리다, 불리는	bullida, bullineun
camera	카메라	kamera
camping	캠핑	kaemping
can opener	깡통 따개	kkangtong ttagae
can, be able to	-(으)ㄹ 수 있다	-(eu)l su itda
can, may	-아/어도 좋다/되다	-a/eodo jota/doeda
cancel, to	취소하다	chwisohada
candle	양초	yangcho
candy, sweets	사탕	satang

cap	모자	*moja*
capable of, to be	-(으)ㄹ 수 있다	*-(eu)l su itda*
car, automobile	자동차	*jadongcha*
car documents	차량 등록증	*charyang deungnokjeung*
car seat (child's)	어린이 보호 좌석	*eorini boho jwaseok*
car trouble	차량 고장	*charyang gojang*
cardigan	카디간	*kadigan*
careful!	조심하세요!	*josimhaseyo!*
carpet	카페트	*kapeteu*
carriage, pram	유모차	*yumocha*
carrot	당근	*danggeun*
cartridge	카트릿지	*kateuritji*
cash, money	현금	*hyeon-geum*
cash card	현금 카드	*hyeon-geum kadeu*
cash desk	계산대	*gyesandae*
cash machine	현금 지급기	*hyeon-geum jigeupgi*
casino	카지노	*kajino*
cassette	카세트	*kaseteu*
cat	고양이	*goyang-i*
catalogue	카달로그	*kadallogeu*
cauliflower	컬리플라워	*keollipeullawo*
cause	원인	*wonin*
cave	동굴	*donggul*
CD	씨디	*ssidi*
CD-ROM	씨디-롬	*ssidi-rom*
celebrate, to	축하하다	chukhahada
cemetery	공동묘지	*gongdongmyoji*
centimetre	센티미터	*sentimiteo*
central heating	중앙 난방	*jung-ang nanbang*
central locking	중앙 잠금 장치	*jung-ang janggeum jangchi*
center (middle)	중앙, 가운데	*jung-ang, gaunde*
center (of city)	(시내) 중심지	*(sinae) jungsimji*
certificate	증명서	*jeungmyeongseo*
chair	• 의자	*uija*
chambermaid	메이드	*meideu*
champagne	샴페인	*syampein*
change (money)	잔돈	*jandon*
change (trains)	바꿔타다	*bakkwotada*
change the baby's diaper/nappy	기저귀를 갈다	*gijeo-gwireul galda*
change the oil	오일을 갈다	*oireul galda*
change, exchange (money), to	환전하다	*hwanjeonhada*
change, swap, to	바꾸다	*bakkuda*
charter flight	전세기 편	*jeonsegi pyeon*
chat, to	이야기하다	*iyagihada*
cheap	싸다, 싼	*ssada, ssan*
check in	체크인하다	*chekeu-inhada*
check out	체크아웃하다	*chekeuauthada*
check, cheque	수표	*supyo*
check, verify, to	체크하다	*chekeuhada*
checked luggage	체크한 여행가방	*chekeuhan yeohaenggabang*
cheers!	건배!	*geonbae!*
cheese	치즈	*chijeu*

English	Korean	Romanization
chef	요리사	yorisa
chess	체스	cheseu
chewing gum	껌	kkeom
chicken	닭(고기)	dak(gogi)
child	아이/ 애, 어린이	ai/ae, eorini
child's seat (in car)	어린이 보호 좌석	eorini boho jwaseok
chilli paste	고추장	gochujang
chin	턱	teok
China	중국	jungguk
chocolate	초콜렛	chokollet
choose, to	선택하다	seontaekhada
chopsticks	젓가락	jeotgarak
Christianity	기독교	gidokgyo
church	교회	gyohoe
church service	예배	yebae
cigar	시가	siga
cigarette	담배	dambae
cinema	극장	geukjang
circus	서커스	seokeoseu
citizen	시민	simin
city	도시	dosi
clean	깨끗하다, 깨끗한	kkaekkeuthada, kkaekkeutan
clean, to	청소하다	cheongsohada
clearance (sale)	세일	seil
climate	기후	gihu
clock	시계	sigye
closed (shop)	끝나다, 끝난	kkeunnada, kkeunnan
closed off (road)	(도로가) 차단되다	(doroga) chadandoeda
cloth	옷감	otgam
clothes dryer	건조기	geonjogi
clothes hanger	옷걸이	otgeori
clothes, clothing	옷	ot
cloudy, overcast	흐리다, 흐린	heurida, heurin
clutch (car)	클러치	keulleochi
coat, overcoat	코트	koteu
cockroach	바퀴벌레	bakwibeolle
cocoa	코코아	kokoa
coffee	커피	keopi
coin	동전	dongjeon
cold (not hot)	춥다, 추운	chupda, chuun
cold, flu	감기	gamgi
collar	칼라	kalla
collarbone	쇄골	swaegol
colleague, co-worker	동료	dongnyo
collide, to	충돌하다	chungdolhada
collision	충돌	chungdol
cologne	화장수	hwajangsu
color	색	saek
comb	빗	bit
come, to	오다	oda
company, firm	회사	hoesa
compartment	칸	kan
complaint	불평	bulpyeong
completely	완전히	wanjeonhi
compliment	칭찬	chingchan

Word list

computer	컴퓨터	keompyuteo
concert	콘서트	konseoteu
concert hall	콘서트 홀	konseoteu hol
concierge	수위	suwi
concussion	뇌진탕	noejintang
condensed milk	연유	yeonyu
condom	콘돔	kondom
confectionery	과자	gwaja
congratulations!	축하해요!	chukhahaeyo!
connection (transport)	연결편	yeon-gyeolpyeon
constipation	변비	byeonbi
consulate	영사관	yeongsa.gwan
consultation (by doctor)	진찰	jinchal
contact lens	콘택트 렌즈	kontaekteu renjeu
contagious	전염되다, 전염되는	jeonyeomdoeda, jeonyeomdoeneun
contraceptive	피임	piim
contraceptive pill	피임약	piimyak
cook (person)	요리사	yorisa
cook, to	요리하다	yorihada
cookie, sweet biscuit	쿠키	kuki
copper	구리	guri
copy	사본, 복사	sabon, boksa
corkscrew	코르크 따개	koreukeu ttagae
corner	코너	koneo
cornflower	옥수수 가루	oksusu garu
correct, to	고치다	gochida
correspond (letters), to	편지 연락하다	pyeonji yeollakhada
corridor	복도	bokdo
cosmetics	화장품	hwajangpum
costume	의상	uisang
cotton	면	myeon
cotton wool	솜	som
cough	기침	gichim
cough syrup	기침 물약	gichim mullyak
cough, to	기침하다	gichimhada
counter (for paying, buying tickets)	카운트	kaunteu
country (nation)	나라	nara
country (rural area)	시골	sigol
country code	국가 번호	gukga beonho
courgettes, zucchini	(애)호박	(ae)hobak
course of treatment	치료	chiryo
cousin	사촌	sachon
crab	게	ge
cracker, salty biscuit	크래커	keuraekeo
cream	크림	keurim
credit card	신용카드	sinyongkadeu
cot, crib	아기 침대	agi chimdae
crime	범죄	beomjoe
crockery	그릇	geureut
cross, angry	화나다, 화난	hwanada, hwanan
cross (road, river), to	건너다	geonneoda
crossroad	교차로	gyocharo
crosswalk, pedestrian crossing	건널목	geonneolmok
crutch	목발	mokbal

cry, to	울다	*ulda*
cubic metre	입방미터	*ipbangmiteo*
cucumber	오이	*oi*
cuddly toy	동물 인형	*dongmul inhyeong*
cuffs	소매단	*somaedan*
cup	컵	*keop*
curly	곱슬하다/-한	*gopseulhada/-han*
current (electric)	전류	*jeollyu*
curtains	커튼	*keoteun*
cushion	쿠션	*kusyeon*
custom (tradition)	관습	*gwanseup*
customs	세관	*segwan*
cut (injury)	상처	*sangcheo*
cut, to	자르다	*jareuda*
cutlery	포크,나이프,스푼	*pokeu,naipeu,seupun*
cycling	자전거 타기	*jajeon-geo tagi*

D

dairy products	유제품	*yujepum*
damage	손해, 손상	*sonhae, sonsang*
dance	춤	*chum*
dance, to	춤추다	*chumchuda*
dandruff	비듬	*bideum*
danger	위험	*wiheom*
dangerous	위험하다, 위험한	*wiheomhada, wiheomhan*
dark	어둡다/진하다, 어두운/진한	*eodupda/jinhada, eoduun/jinhan*
date (of the month)	날짜	*naljja*
date of birth	생년월일	*saengnyeonworil*
daughter	딸	*ttal*
day	날, 낮	*nal, nat*
day after tomorrow	모레	*more*
day before yesterday	그저께	*geujeokke*
dead	죽다, 죽은	*jukda, jugeun*
deaf	귀가 먹다/먹은	*gwiga meokda/meogeun*
decaffeinated	카페인 없는	*kapein eomneun*
December	십이월	*sibiwol*
declare (customs)	신고	*sin-go*
deep	깊다, 깊은	*gipda, gipeun*
deep freeze, freezer	냉동고	*naengdonggo*
deep-sea diving	스킨 다이빙	*seukin daibing*
defecate, to	배설하다	*baeseolhada*
degrees (temperature)	도	*do*
delay	지연	*jiyeon*
delicious	맛있다, 맛있는	*masitda, masinneun*
dentist	치과(의사)	*chikkwa(uisa)*
dentures	틀니	*teulli*
deodorant	탈취제	*talchwije*
department store	백화점	*baekhwajeom*
departure	출발	*chulbal*
depilatory cream	탈모제	*talmoje*
deposit (for safekeeping), to	보관하다	*bo-gwanhada*
deposit (in the bank), to	예금하다	*yegeumhada*
desert (arid land)	사막	*samak*

Word list

15

dessert	디저트	dijeoteu
destination	목적지	mokjeokji
detergent	세제	seje
develop (film), to	현상하다	hyeonsanghada
diabetic	당뇨병 환자	dangnyobyeong hwanja
dial (telephone), to	전화하다	jeonhwahada
diamond	다이아몬드	daiamondeu
diaper	기저귀	gojeo-gwi
diarrhoea	설사	seolsa
dictionary	사전	sajeon
diesel oil	디젤유	dijellyu
diet	식이요법	sigiyobeop
difficulty	어려움	eoryeoum
dining car	식당칸	sikdangkan
dining room	식당	sikdang
dinner, evening meal	저녁 식사	jeonyeok siksa
direct flight	직항	jikhang
direction	방향	banghyang
directly	직접	jikjeop
dirty	더럽다, 더러운	deoreopda, deoreo.un
disabled person	장애인	jang-aein
discount	디스카운트	diseukaunteu
discuss, to	의논하다	uinonhada
discussion	의논	uinon
dish (particular food)	요리	yori
dish of the day	오늘의 스페셜	oneurui seupesyeol
disinfectant	소독제	sodokje
dislike, to	싫어하다	sireohada
distance	거리	geori
distilled water	증류수	jeungnyusu
disturb, to	방해하다	banghaehada
disturbance	방해	banghae
dive, to	다이빙하다	daibinghada
diving	다이빙	daibing
diving board	다이빙 보드	daibing bodeu
diving gear	다이빙 장비	daibing jangbi
divorced	이혼하다, 이혼한	ihonhada, ihonhan
dizzy	어지럽다, 어지러운	eojireopda, eojireoun
do not disturb	방해하지 마세요.	banghaehaji maseyo.
do, perform an action, to	하다	hada
doctor	의사	uisa
dog	개	gae
doll	인형	inhyeong
domestic (flight)	국내선	gungnaeseon
don't!	그러지 마세요!	geureoji maseyo!
done (cooked)	잘 익다, 잘 익은	jal ikda, jal igeun
door	문	mun
double	두 배	du bae
down, downward	아래로	araero
drapes, curtains	커튼	keoteun
dream, to	꿈꾸다	kkumkkuda
dress, frock	드레스	deureseu
dressing gown	실내복	sillaebok
dressing table	화장대	hwajangdae
drink (alcoholic)	술	sul
drink (refreshment)	음료(수)	eumnyo(su)

drink, to	마시다	*masida*
drinking water	식수	*siksu*
drive (a car), to	운전하다	*unjeonhada*
driver	운전사	*unjeonsa*
driver's license	운전 면허증	*unjeon myeonheojjeung*
drugstore, pharmacy	약국	*yakguk*
drunk	술 취하다	*sul chwihada*
dry	마르다, 마른	*mareuda, mareun*
dry, to	말리다	*mallida*
dry-clean	드라이 클리닝	*deurai keullining*
dry cleaners	세탁소	*setakso*
duck	오리	*ori*
during, for	...동안	*...dong-an*
duty (import tax)	관세	*gwanse*
duty-free goods	면세품	*myeonsepum*
duty-free shop	면세점	*myeonsejeom*
DVD	디비디	*dibidi*

E

ear	귀	*gwi*
ear drops	귀 물약	*gwi mullyak*
earache	이통	*itong*
early	이르다, 이른	*ireuda, ireun*
earrings	귀걸이	*gwigeori*
earth, soil	흙	*heuk*
earthenware	도기	*dogi*
east	동쪽	*dongjjok*
easy	쉽다, 쉬운	*swipda, swiun*
eat, to	먹다	*meokda*
economy class	이코노미석	*ikonomiseok*
eczema	습진	*seupjin*
eel	장어	*jang-eo*
egg	계란, 알	*gyeran, al*
eggplant, aubergine	가지	*gaji*
electric	전기(의)	*jeon-gi(ui)*
electricity	전기	*jeon-gi*
electronic	전자(의)	*jeonja(ui)*
elephant	코끼리	*kokkiri*
elevator	엘리베이터	*ellibeiteo*
email (message)	이 메일	*i meil*
embassy	대사관	*daesagwan*
embroidery	(자)수	*(ja)su*
emergency	응급(사태)	*eunggeup(satae)*
emergency brake	비상 브레이크	*bisang beureikeu*
emergency exit	비상구	*bisanggu*
emergency phone	응급 전화	*eunggeup jeonhwa*
emergency room	응급실	*eunggeupsil*
empty	텅 비다/빈	*teong bida/bin*
engaged (telephone)	통화중이다/-중인	*tonghwajung-ida/-jung-in*
engaged (to be married)	약혼하다/-한	*yakonhada/-han*
England	영국	*yeongguk*
English	영어	*yeong-eo*
enjoy, to	즐기다	*jeulgida*
enquire, to	물어보다	*mureoboda*
envelope	봉투	*bongtu*

escalator	에스컬레이터	eseukeolleiteo
essential	필수적이다, 필수적인	pilsujeogida, pilsujeogin
evening	저녁	jeonyeok
evening wear	야회복	yahoebok
event	행사	haengsa
every	모든, 매..	modeun, mae...
everybody, everyone	모든 사람	modeun saram
everything	모든 것	modeun geot
everywhere	어디든지, 모든 곳	eodideunji, modeun got
examine, to	검토하다, 진찰하다	geomtohada, jinchalhada
excavation	발굴	balgul
excellent	우수하다, 우수한	usuhada, usuhan
exchange (money, opinions), to	교환하다	gyohwanhada
exchange office	환전소	hwanjeonso
exchange rate	환율	hwannyul
excuse me!	실례합니다!	sillyehamnida!
excuse me! (apology)	미안합니다!	mianhamnida!
exhibition	전시회	jeonsihoe
exit, way out	출구	chulgu
expense	비용	biyong
expensive	비싸다, 비싼	bissada, bissan
explain, to	설명하다	seolmyeonghada
express, state, to	표현하다	pyohyeonhada
eye	눈	nun
eye drops	눈약	nunyak
eye specialist	안과 전문의	ankkwa jeonmun-ui

F

fabric, textile	직물	jingmul
face	얼굴	eolgul
factory	공장	gongjang
fall (season)	가을	ga-eul
fall over, to	넘어지다	neomeojida
family	가족	gajok
famous	유명하다, 유명한	yumyeonghada, yumyeonghan
fan (admirer)	팬	paen
fan (for cooling)	부채	buchae
far away	멀다, 먼	meolda, meon
farm	농장	nongjang
farmer	농부	nongbu
fashion	패션	paesyeon
fast, rapid	빠르다, 빠른	ppareuda, ppareun
father	아버지	abeoji
father-in-law	시아버지, 장인	siabeoji, jang.in
fault	잘못	jalmot
fax	팩스	paekseu
fax, to	팩스 보내다	paekseu bonaeda
February	이월	iwol
feel like	-고 싶다	-go sipda
feel, to	느끼다	neukkida
female	여성	yeoseong
fence	담, 울타리	dam, ultari

ferry	배	*bae*
fever	열	*yeol*
fiancé	약혼자	*yakonja*
fiancée	약혼녀	*yakonnyeo*
fill out (form), to	작성하다	*jakseonghada*
fill, to	채우다	*chae.uda*
film (camera)	필름	*pilleum*
filter	필터	*pilteo*
fine (good)	좋다, 좋은	*jota, jo-eun*
fine (money)	벌금	*beolgeum*
finger	손가락	*sonkkarak*
fire	불	*bul*
fire alarm	화재 경보	*hwajae gyeongbo*
fire department, fire service	소방서	*sobangseo*
fire escape	비상구	*bisanggu*
fire extinguisher	소화기	*sohwagi*
first	첫 번째	*cheot beonjjae*
first aid	응급 조치	*eunggeup jochi*
first class	일등석	*ildeungseok*
fish	물고기, 생선	*mulkkogi (live), saengseon (food)*
fishing	낚시	*naksi*
fishing rod	낚싯대	*naksitdae*
fitness club	헬스 클럽	*helseu keulleop*
fitness training	체력 단련	*cheryeok dallyeon*
fitting room	탈의실	*taruisil*
fix (repair), to	고치다	*gochida*
flag	깃발	*gitbal*
flash (camera)	플래쉬	*peullaeswi*
flashlight, torch	손전등	*sonjeondeung*
flatulence	복부 팽만	*bokbu paengman*
flavor	맛	*mat*
flavoring	첨가물	*cheomgamul*
flea	벼룩	*byeoruk*
flea market	벼룩시장	*byeoruksijang*
flight	운항	*unhang*
flight number	운항 번호	*unhang beonho*
flood	홍수	*hongsu*
floor	마루, 층	*maru, cheung*
flour	밀가루	*milkkaru*
flower	꽃	*kkot*
flu	독감	*dokgam*
flush (toilet), to	변기 물을 내리다	*byeon.gi mureul naerida*
fly (insect)	파리	*pari*
fly, to	날다	*nalda*
fog	안개	*an.gae*
foggy	안개끼다, 안개낀	*an.gaekkida, an.gaekkin*
folklore	민담	*mindam*
follow behind, to	뒤따라가다	*dwittaragada*
food (meal)	음식	*eumsik*
food court	음식 백화점	*eumsik baekhwajeom*
food poisoning	식중독	*sikjungdok*
foot	발	*bal*
foot brake	발 브레이크	*bal beureikeu*

121

forbidden	금지되다, 금지된	*geumjidoeda, geumjidoen*
forehead	이마	*ima*
foreign	외국(의)	*oeguk(ui)*
foreigner	외국인	*oegugin*
forget, to	잊어버리다	*ijeobeorida*
fork	포크	*pokeu*
form (application)	신청서	*sincheongseo*
form (to fill out), to	작성하다	*jakseonghada*
formal dress	정장	*jeongjang*
fountain	분수	*bunsu*
frame (photo)	액자	*aekja*
free (no charge)	무료(의)	*muryo(ui)*
free (unoccupied)	비어있다, 비어있는	*bieo-itda, bieo-inneun*
free time	자유시간	*jayusigan*
freeze, to	얼(리)다	*eol(li)da*
french fries	감자 튀김	*gamja twigim*
fresh	신선하다, 신선한	*sinseonhada, sinseonhan*
Friday	금요일	*geumyoil*
fried	튀긴	*twigin*
friend	친구	*chin.gu*
friendly	친절하다, 친절한	*chinjeolhada, chinjeolhan*
frightened	겁먹다, 겁먹은	*geommeokda, geommeogeun*
fringe (hair)	앞머리	*ammeori*
frozen	얼다, 언	*eolda, eon*
fruit	과일	*gwail*
fruit juice	과일 주스	*gwail juseu*
frying pan	프라이팬	*peuraipaen*
full	가득 차다/찬	*gadeuk chada, gadeuk chan*
fun, to have	재미있게 보내다	*jaemiitge bonaeda*
funeral	장례식	*jangnyesik*

G

gallery	화랑	*hwarang*
game	게임	*geim*
garage (for repairs)	정비소	*jeongbiso*
garbage	쓰레기	*sseuregi*
garden, yard	정원	*jeong-won*
garlic	마늘	*maneul*
garment	옷	*ot*
gas (for heating)	가스	*gaseu*
gas station	주유소	*juyuso*
gasoline	가솔린	*gasollin*
gasoline station	주유소	*juyuso*
gate	문	*mun*
gear (car)	기어	*gieo*
gem	보석	*boseok*
gender	성별	*seongbyeol*
genuine	진짜(의)	*jinjja(ui)*
germ	세균	*se-gyun*
get off (transport), to	내리다	*naerida*
get on (transport) , to	타다	*tada*
gift	선물	*seonmul*

ginger	생강	*saenggang*
girl	소녀	*so.nyeo*
girlfriend	여자 친구	*yeoja chin-gu*
give, to	주다	*juda*
given name	이름	*ireum*
glad	기쁘다, 기쁜	*gippeuda, gippeun*
glass (for drinking)	컵	*keop*
glass (material)	유리	*yuri*
glasses, spectacles	안경	*an-gyeong*
gliding	글라이딩	*geullaiding*
glossy (photo)	광택지	*gwangtaekji*
gloves	장갑	*janggap*
glue	풀	*pul*
gnat	모기	*mogi*
go back , to	돌아가다	*doragada*
go out, exit, to	나가다	*nagada*
go to bed, to	자다/ 자러가다	*jada/jareogada*
go, to	가다	*gada*
gold	금	*geum*
golf	골프	*golpeu*
golf course	골프장	*golpeujang*
good	좋다, 좋은	*jota, jo-eun*
good afternoon	안녕하세요.	*annyeonghaseyo*
good evening	안녕하세요.	*annyeonghaseyo*
good luck!	행운을 빕니다!	*haeng-uneul bimnida!*
good morning	안녕하세요.	*annyeonghaseyo*
good night	안녕히 주무세요.	*annyeonghi jumuseyo*
goodbye (to a person leaving)	안녕히 가세요	*annyeonghi gaseyo*
goodbye (to a person staying)	안녕히 계세요	*annyeonghi gyeseyo*
grade crossing. level crossing	철도 건널목	*cheoldo geonneolmok*
gram	그램	*graem*
grammar	문법	*munbeop*
grandchild	손자(M), 손녀(F)	*sonja(M), sonnyeo(F)*
granddaughter	손녀	*sonnyeo*
grandfather	할아버지, 조부	*harabeoji, jobu*
grandmother	할머니, 조모	*halmeoni, jomo*
grandparents	조부모	*jobumo*
grandson	손자	*sonja*
grape juice	포도 주스	*podo juseu*
grapes	포도	*podo*
grave	무덤	*mudeom*
graze (injury)	찰과상	*chalgwasang*
greasy	기름기 많다, 기름기 많은	*gireumkki manta, gireumkki maneun*
green	푸르다, 푸른	*pureuda, pureun*
greengrocer	야채	*yachae*
greet, to	인사하다	*insahada*
greetings	인사말	*insamal*
grey	회색(의)	*hoesaek(ui)*
grey-haired	백발의	*baekbarui*
grilled	굽다, 구운	*gupda, guun*
grocery	식품점	*sikpumjeom*
groceries	식품	*sikpum*

Word list

15

123

group	그룹	geurup
guest	손님	sonnim
guest house	여관	yeogwan
guide (book)	안내서	annaeseo
guide (person)	가이드	gaideu
guided tour	가이드가 있는 투어	gaideuga inneun tueo
guilty, to feel	죄책감을 느끼다	joechaekgameul neukkida
gym	짐	jim
gynaecologist	산부인과 의사	sanbu-inkkwa uisa

H

hair	머리(카락)	meori(karak)
hairbrush	빗	bit
haircut	컷트	keoteu
hairdresser	미용사	miyongsa
hair dryer	헤어 드라이어	he-eo deuraieo
hair spray	헤어 스프레이	he-eo seupeurei
hair style	헤어 스타일	he-eo seutail
half	반	ban
half full	반	ban
hammer	망치	mangchi
hand	손	son
hand brake	손 브레이크	son beureikeu
hand luggage	휴대 수하물	hyudae suhamul
hand towel	손 타월	son tawol
handbag	핸드백	haendeubaek
handkerchief	손수건	sonsugeon
handmade	수공	sugong
happy	행복하다, 행복한	haengbokhada, hangbokan
happy birthday!	생일 축하합니다!	saeng-il chukhahamnida!
happy new year!	새해 복 많이 받으세요!	saehae bok mani badeuseyo!
harbor	항구	hanggu
hard (difficult)	어렵다, 어려운	eoryeopda, eoryeo-un
hard (firm)	단단하다, 단단한	dandanhada, dandanhan
hardware store	철물점	cheolmuljeom
hat	모자	moja
have to, must	-아/어야 하다	-a/eoya hada
have, own, to	있다	itda
hay fever	꽃가루 알레르기	kkotgaru allereugi
he, him	그	geu
head	머리	meori
headache	두통	dutong
headlights	헤드 라이트	hedeu raiteu
health food shop	건강 식품점	geon-gang sikpumjeom
healthy	건강하다, 건강한	geon-ganghada, geon-ganghan
hear, to	듣다	deutda
hearing aid	보청기	bocheonggi
heart	심장, 마음	simjang, ma-eum
heart attack	심장 마비	simjang mabi
heat, to	데우다	de-uda

heater	히터	hiteo
heavy	무겁다, 무거운	mugeopda, mugeo.un
heel (of foot)	발꿈치	balkkumchi
heel (of shoe)	굽	gup
hello! (on phone)	여보세요!	yeoboseyo!
hello, hi	안녕하세요	annyeonghaseyo
help!	도와주세요!	dowajuseyo!
help yourself	마음대로 드세요	ma-eumdaero deuseyo
hem	단	dan
her	그녀의	geunyeo.ui
herbal tea	허브 차	heobeu cha
herbs	허브	heobeu
here	여기, 이리(로)	yeogi, iri(ro)
hers	그녀의 것	geunyeo-ui geot
high	높다, 높은	nopda, nopeun
high chair	애기용 식탁의자	aegiyong siktakuija
high tide	밀물	milmul
highway	고속도로	gosokdoro
hiking	등산	deungsan
hiking boots	등산화	deungsanhwa
hip	힙	hip
hire, to	고용하다	goyonghada
his	그의, 그의 것	geu-ui, geu-ui geot
hitchhike	히치 하이크	hichi haikeu
hobby	취미	chwimi
holiday (public)	휴일	hyu-il
holiday (vacation)	휴가	hyuga
home, house	집	jip
homesickness	향수병	hyangsuppyeong
honest	정직하다, 정직한	jeongjikhada, jeongjikan
honey	꿀	kkul
horizontal	수평이다, 수평인	supyeong-ida, supyeong-in
horrible	형편없다, 형편없는	hyeongpyeoneopda, hyeongpyeoneomneun
horse	말	mal
hospital	병원	byeong-won
hospitality (friendly)	환대	hwandae
hot (spicy)	맵다, 매운	maepda, mae-un
hot (temperature)	덥다, 더운	deopda, deo-un
hot spring	온천	oncheon
hot-water bottle	보온병	boonbyeong
hotel	호텔	hotel
hour	시간	sigan
house	집	jip
how are you?	안녕하세요?	annyeonghaseyo?
how far?	얼마나 멀어요	eolmana meoreoyo?
how long?	얼마나 오래요?	eolmana oraeyo?
how many?	얼마나 많이요?	eolmana maniyo?
how much?	얼마예요?	eolmayeyo?
how old?	몇 살이에요?	myeot sarieyo?
how?	어떻게요?	eotteokeyo?
however	그러나	geureona
humid	무덥다, 무더운	mudeopda, mudeo.un

English	Korean	Romanization
hundred grams	백 그램	baekgeuraem
hungry	배고프다, 배고픈	baegopeuda, baegopeun
hurry up!	빨리요!	ppalliyo!
husband	남편	nampyeon
hut, shack	오두막	odumak

I

English	Korean	Romanization
I, me	나, 내, 저, 제	na, nae, jeo, je
ice cream	아이스 크림	aiseu keurim
ice cubes	얼음 조각	eoreum jogak
ice-skating	아이스 스케이팅	aiseu seukeiting
iced	얼다, 언	eolda, eon
idea	생각	saenggak
identification (card)	신분증	sinbunjjeung
if	만일 -(으)면	manil -(eu)myeon
ignition key	차 열쇠	cha yeolsoe
ill, sick	아프다, 아픈	apeuda, apeun
illness	병	byeong
imagine, to	상상하다	sangsanghada
immediately	곧	got
import duty	관세	gwanse
important	중요하다, 중요한	jung-yohada, jung-yohan
impossible	불가능하다/-한	bulganeunghada/-han
in order that, so that	-기 위해서	-gi wihaeseo
in the evening	저녁에	jeo-nyeoge
in the morning	아침에	achime
in, at (place)	...에(서)	...e(seo)
in-laws	처가 사람, 시댁 사람	cheoga saram, sidaek saram
included	포함되다, 포함된,	pohamdoeda, pohamdoen,
including	포함하다, 포함하는	pohamhada, pohamhaneun
indicate, to	가리키다	garikida
indicator (car)	깜박이 등	kkambagi deung
indigestion	소화불량	sohwabullyang
inexpensive	싸다, 싼	ssada, ssan
infection	감염	gamyeom
infectious	전염되다, 전염되는	jeonyeomdoeda, jeonyeomdoeneun
inflammation	염증	yeomjjeung
information	정보, 안내	jeongbo, annae
information office	안내소	annaeso
injection	주사	jusa
injured	다치다, 다친	dachida, dachin
innocent	결백하다, 결백한	gyeolbaekada, gyeolbaekan
insane	미치다, 미친	michida, michin
insect	벌레	beolle
insect bite	벌레 물린 상처	beolle mullin sangcheo
insect repellent	방충제	bangchungje
inside	안쪽	anjjok
instructions	사용 설명서	sayong seolmyeongseo

insurance	보험	*boheom*
interested in	관심이 있다/ 있는	*gwansimi itda/inneun*
interesting	재미있다, 재미있는	*jaemiitda,*
		jaemiinneun
intermission	중간 휴식	*junggan hyusik*
internal	내부의	*naebuui*
Internet café	인터넷 카페	*inteonet kape*
interpreter	통역(사)	*tong-yeok(sa)*
intersection	교차(로)	*gyocha(ro)*
interview	면접	*myeonjeop*
introduce someone, to	소개하다	*sogaehada*
invent, to	발명하다	*balmyeonghada*
invite, to	초대하다	*chodaehada*
invoice	청구서	*cheongguseo*
iodine	요오드	*yoodeu*
Ireland	아일랜드	*aillaendeu*
iron (metal)	철	*cheol*
iron (clothing), to	다리다	*darida*
ironing board	다림질판	*darimjilpan*
island	섬	*seom*
itch	가려움증	*garyeoumjjeung*

J

jack (for car)	잭	*jaek*
jacket	자켓	*jaket*
jam	잼	*jaem*
January	일월	*irwol*
Japan	일본	*ilbon*
jaw	턱	*teok*
jeans	진	*jin*
jellyfish	해파리	*haepari*
jeweller	보석상	*boseoksang*
jewellery	보석	*boseok*
job	직업, 일	*jigeop, il*
jog, to	조깅하다	*joginghada*
joke	농담	*nongdam*
journey	여행	*yeohaeng*
juice	쥬스	*jyuseu*
July	칠월	*chirwol*
June	유월	*yuwol*

K

kerosene	등유	*deungyu*
key (to room)	열쇠	*yeolsoe*
kidney	신장	*sinjang*
kilogram	킬로그램	*killogeuraem*
king	왕	*wang*
kiss	키스	*kiseu*
kiss, to	키스하다	*kiseuhada*
kitchen	부엌	*bu-eok*
knee	무릎	*mureup*
knife	칼	*kal*
knit	니트	*niteu*
know, to	알다	*alda*
Korea, North	북한	*bukhan*
Korea, South	남한	*namhan*

Word list

15

127

Korean	한국 사람, 한국어	han-guk saram, han-gugeo

L

lace (fabric)	레이스	reiseu
laces (for shoes)	신발 끈	sinbal kkeun
ladder	사다리	sadari
lake	호수	hosu
lamb, mutton	양고기	yanggogi
lamp	등	deung
land (ground)	땅	ttang
land (plane), to	착륙하다	changnyukhada
lane (of traffic)	차선	chaseon
language	말, 언어	mal, eoneo
large	크다, 큰	keuda, keun
last (endure)	오래가다	oraegada
last (final)	마지막이다, 마지막	majimagida, majimak
last night	지난 밤	jinan bam
later	나중에	najung-e
laugh, to	웃다	utda
launderette	빨래방	ppallaebang
laundry	세탁소	setakso
laundry soap	세탁 비누	setak binu
law, legislation	법	beop
lawyer	변호사	byeonhosa
laxative	완화제	wanhwaje
leak, to	새다	saeda
leather	가죽	gajuk
leather goods	가죽 제품	gajuk jepum
leave, depart, to	떠나다	tteonada
left behind	남다	namda
left-hand side	왼쪽	oenjjok
leg	다리	dari
leggings	레깅즈	regingjeu
leisure	레저	rejeo
lemon, citrus	레몬	remon
lend, to	빌려주다	billyeojuda
lens (camera)	렌즈	renjeu
less (smaller amount)	더 적다/ 적은	deo jeokda/jeogeun
lesson	수업, 강습	su-eop, gangseup
letter	편지	pyeonji
lettuce	양상치	yangsangchi
level crossing, grade crossing	철도 건널목	cheoldo geonneolmok
library	도서관	doseogwan
license (for driving)	면 허증	myeonheojjeung
lie (falsehood)	거짓말	geojinmal
lie down, to	눕다	nupda
lift (elevator)	엘리베이터	ellibeiteo
lift (in car), to give	태워주다	taewojuda
light (lamp)	불	bul
light (not dark)	밝다/연하다, 밝은/연한	baltta/yeonhada, balgeun/yeonhan
light (not heavy)	가볍다, 가벼운	gabyeopda, gabyeo.un
light bulb	전구	jeongu
lighter	라이터	raiteo
lightning	번개	beon.gae

Word list

15

like, be pleased by, to	좋아하다	joahada
line (mark)	선	seon
line (queue)	줄	jul
linen (fiber)	린넨	rinnen
lining	안감	ankkam
liquor store	주류상	juryusang
liquor, alcohol	술	sul
listen, to	듣다	deutda
literature	문학	munhak
litre	리터	riteo
little (amount)	적다, 적은	jeokda, jeogeun
little (small)	작다, 작은	jakda, jageun
live (be alive)	살아있는	sarainneun
live, to	살다	salda
liver	간	gan
lobster	롭스터	ropseuteo
local	지역	jiyeok
lock	자물쇠	jamulsoe
long (length)	길다, 긴	gilda, gin
look at, see, to	보다	boda
look for, to	찾다	chatda
look up (find in book), to	찾아보다	chajaboda
lose, mislay, to	잃어버리다	ireobeorida
loss (profit)	손실	sonsil
lost (can't find way)	길을 잃다/잃은	gireul ilta/ireun
lost (missing)	잃어버린	ireobeorin
lost and found office	분실물 센터	bunsilmul senteo
lotion	로션	rosyeon
loud	소리가 크다/ 큰	soriga keuda/keun
love	사랑	sarang
love, to	사랑하다	saranghada
low	낮다, 낮은	natda, najeun
low tide	썰물	sseolmul
LPG	엘피지	elpiji
luck	운	un
luggage	여행가방	yeohaenggabang
luggage locker	보관함	bogwanham
lumps (sugar)	각설탕	gakseoltang
lunch	점심 식사	jeomsim siksa
lungs	폐	pye

M

madam (term of address)	부인	bu.in
magazine	잡지	japji
mail, post	우편물	upyeonmul
mail, to	부치다	buchida
main post office	중앙 우체국	jung-ang ucheguk
main road	대로	daero
make an appointment	약속하다	yaksokhada
make love	섹스하다	sekseuhada
make, create, to	만들다	mandeulda
makeshift	임시	imsi
makeup	화장	hwajang
male	남성	namseong
man	남자	namja
manager	관리 책임자	gwalli chaegimja
mango	망고	manggo

manicure	손톱 손질	sontop sonjil
many, much	많다, 많은	manta, maneun
map	지도	jido
marble	대리석	daeriseok
March	삼월	samwol
margarine	마아가린	maagarin
marina (for yachts)	정박소	jeongbakso
marital status	결혼 여부	gyeolhon yeobu
market	시장	sijang
married	결혼하다, 결혼한	gyeolhonhada, gyeolhonhan
massage, to	마사지하다	massajihada
mat (on floor)	깔개	kkalgae
mat (on table)	받침	batchim
match, game	시합	sihap
matches	성냥	seongnyang
matte (photo)	매트지	maeteuji
may	-아/어도 좋다	-a/eodo jota
May	오월	owol
maybe	아마	ama
mayonnaise	마요네즈	mayonejeu
mayor	시장	sijang
meal	식사	siksa
mean (word), to	의미하다	uimihada
meaning	의미	uimi
measure out, to	재다	jaeda
measuring jug	계량컵	gyeryangkeop
meat	고기	gogi
medicine	약	yak
meet, to	만나다	mannada
melon	참외	chamoe
member	회원	hoewon
member of parliament	국회의원	gukoe-uiwon
membership card	회원권	hoewonkkwon
mend, to	고치다	gochida
menstruate, to	생리하다	saengnihada
menstruation	생리	saengni
menu	메뉴	menyu
message	메시지	messiji
metal	금속	geumsok
meter (in taxi)	미터기	miteogi
metre	미터	miteo
migraine	편두통	pyeondutong
mild (taste)	순하다, 순한	sunhada, sunhan
milk	우유	uyu
millimeter	밀리미터	millimiteo
mind, be displeased, to	신경 쓰이다	sin-gyeong sseuida
mine	내 것, 제 것	nae geot, je geot
mineral water	광천수	gwangcheonsu
minute	분	bun
mirror	거울	geo.ul
miss (flight, train), to	놓치다	nochida
miss (loved one), to	보고싶다, 보고싶어하다	bogosipda, bogosipeohada
missing	없어지다, 없어진	eopseojida, eopseojin
mist	안개	angae
mistake	실수	silsu

mistaken	틀리다, 틀린	*teullida, teullin*
misty	뿌옇다, 뿌연	*ppuyeota, ppuyeon*
misunderstanding	오해	*ohae*
mixed	섞이다, 섞인	*seokkida, seokkin*
mobile phone	핸드폰	*haendeupon*
modern art	현대 미술	*hyeondae misul*
moment (instant)	순간	*sun-gan*
Monday	월요일	*woryoil*
money	돈	*don*
monkey	원숭이	*wonsung-i*
month	달	*dal*
moon	달	*dal*
moped	모터 자전거	*moteo jajeongeo*
more (comparative)	더	*deo*
morning	아침	*achim*
mosquito	모기	*mogi*
mosquito net	모기장	*mogijang*
most (superlative)	가장	*gajang*
motel	모델	*motel*
mother	어머니	*eomeoni*
mother-in-law	시어머니, 장모	*sieomeoni, jangmo*
motorbike	오토바이	*otobai*
motorboat	모터 보트	*moteo boteu*
mountain	산	*san*
mountain hut	산장	*sanjang*
mouse (animal)	생쥐	*saengjwi*
moustache	콧수염	*kossuyeom*
mouth	입	*ip*
movie	영화	*yeonghwa*
MSG	조미료	*jomiryo*
much, many	많다, 많은	*manta, maneun*
mud	진흙	*jinheuk*
muscle	근육	*geunyuk*
muscle spasms	근육 경련	*geunyuk gyeongnyeon*
museum	박물관	*bangmulgwan*
mushroom	버섯	*beoseot*
music	음악	*eumak*
must	-아/어야 하다	*-a/eoya hada*
my	내, 제	*nae, je*

N

nail (finger, toe)	손톱, 발톱	*sontop, baltop*
nail (spike)	못	*mot*
nail file	손톱 줄	*sontopjul*
nail scissors	손톱 가위	*sontop gawi*
naked	벌거벗다/-벗은	*beolgeobeotda/ -beoseun*
name	이름	*ireum*
nappy, diaper	기저귀	*gijeo.gwi*
nationality	국적	*gukjeok*
natural	자연(적인)	*jayeon(jeogin)*
nature	자연	*jayeon*
nauseous	메스껍다, 메스꺼운	*meseukkeopda, meseukkeoun*
near	가까이	*gakkai*
nearby	가까이에	*gakkaie*

Word list

15

necessary	필요하다, 필요한	*piryohada, piryohan*
neck	목	*mok*
necklace	목걸이	*mokgeori*
necktie	넥타이	*nektai*
need, to	필요하다	*piryohada*
needle	바늘	*baneul*
negative (photo)	네가티브	*negatibeu*
neighbor	이웃(사람)	*iut(saram)*
nephew	조카	*joka*
never	결코...아니다/	*gyeolko ...anida/*
	-지 않다	*-ji anta*
new	새롭다, 새(로운)	*saeropda, sae(roun)*
news	뉴스	*nyuseu*
news stand	신문 가판대	*sinmun gapandae*
newspaper	신문	*sinmun*
next (in line, sequence)	다음(의)	*da.eum(ui)*
next to	...옆에	*...yeope*
nice	멋지다, 멋진	*meotjida, meotjin*
nice (pleasant)	기분 좋다, 기분 좋은	*gibun jota,*
		gibun jo.eun
niece	조카딸	*jokattal*
night	밤	*bam*
night duty	야간 근무	*yagan geunmu*
night clothes	잠옷	*jamot*
nightclub	나이트 클럽	*naiteu keuleop*
nightdress	잠옷	*jamot*
nipple (bottle)	젖꼭지	*jeotkkokji*
no (answer)	아뇨	*anyo*
no entry	진입금지	*jinipgeumji*
no thank you	괜찮아요	*gwaenchanayo*
no, not (with nouns)	...아니다	*...anida*
no, not (with verbs and adjectives)	안, -지 않다	*an, -ji anta*
no-one	아무도 ...아니다/	*amudo ...anida/*
	-지 않다	*-ji anta*
noise	소음	*so-eum*
nonstop (flight)	직항	*jikang*
noodles	국수	*guksu*
normal	정상적이다/-적인	*jeongsangjeogida,*
		jeongsangjeogin
north	북쪽	*bukjjok*
nose	코	*ko*
nosebleed	코피	*kopi*
notebook	노트, 공책	*noteu, gongchaek*
notepad	노트, 공책	*noteu, gongchaek*
notepaper	편지지	*pyeonjiji*
nothing	아무것도 ...아니다	*amugeotdo ...anida*
November	십일월	*sibirwol*
now	지금	*jigeum*
nowhere	어디에도 ...없다	*eodiedo ...eopda*
number	숫자, 번호	*sutja, beonho*
number plate	번호판	*beonopan*
nurse	간호사	*ganhosa*
nuts	밤, 호두	*bam, hodu*

O

o'clock	...시	*...si*

object, thing	물체, 사물	mulche, samul
occupation	직업	jigeop
October	시월	siwol
off (gone bad)	상하다	sanghada
off (turned off)	꺼져 있다	kkeojyeo itda
offer, suggest, to	제의하다	je-uihada
office	사무실	samusil
often	자주	jaju
oil	기름	gireum
ointment	연고	yeon-go
okay	좋다, 괜찮다	jota, gwaenchanta
old (of persons)	나이 많다/많은	nai manta/maneun
on (turned on)	켜져 있다	kyeojyeo itda
on board	타고 있다	tago itda
on foot	걸어서	georeoseo
on the left	왼쪽에	oenjjoge
on the right	오른쪽에	oreunjjoge
on the way	오는/ 가는 길에	oneun/ganeun gire
oncoming car	맞은편에 오는 차량	majeunpyeone
		oneun charyang
one-way ticket	편도표	pyeondopyo
one-way traffic	일방통행	ilbangtonghaeng
onion	양파	yangpa
open	열리다, 열린	yeollida, yeollin
open, to	열다	yeolda
operate (surgeon), to	수술하다	susulhada
operator (telephone)	교환	gyohwan
opposite (contrary)	반대(의)	bandae(ui)
optician	안경사, 안경점	angyeongsa,
		angyeongjeom
or	또는	ttoneun
orange (color)	오렌지색	orenjisaek
orange (fruit)	오렌지	orenji
order (command)	주문	jumun
order something, to	주문하다	jumunhada
other	다른	dareun
other side	다른 쪽	dareun jjok
our	우리(의)	uri(ui)
outside	바깥(쪽)	bakkat(jjok)
outside of	...의 바깥에	...ui bakkate
over there	저기(로)	jeogi(ro)
overcome, to	이겨내다	igyeonaeda
overpass, flyover	고가도로	gogadoro
overseas	해외(의)	hae.oe(ui)
overtake, to	추월하다	chuwolhada
oyster	굴	gul

P

packed lunch	도시락	dosirak
page	페이지	peiji
pain	통증	tongjjeung
painful	아프다, 아픈	apeuda, apeun
painkiller	진통제	jintongje
paint	페인트	peinteu
painting	그림, 칠	geurim, chil
pajamas	파자마	pajama
palace	궁	gung

pan	냄비	naembi
pane	창유리	changyuri
panties	팬티	paenti
pants	바지	baji
pantyhose	팬티 스타킹	panti seutaking
paper	종이	jong-i
parasol	파라솔	parasol
parcel	소포	sopo
pardon me?	뭐라고 하셨어요?	mworago hasyeosseoyo?
parents	부모	bumo
park (car), to	주차하다	juchahada
park, gardens	공원	gong-won
parking garage	차고	chago
parking space	주차장	juchajang
parliament	국회	gukhoe
part (of machine)	부속	busok
partner (in business)	동업자	dong-eopja
partner (spouse)	배우자	bae-uja
party (event)	파티	pati
passenger	승객	seunggaek
passport	여권	yeokkwon
passport photo	여권 사진	yeokkwon sajin
patient (calm)	인내심 있다/-있는	innaesimitda/-inneun
patient (doctor's)	환자	hwanja
pay (bill), to	지불하다	jibulhada
peach	복숭아	boksung-a
peanut	땅콩	ttangkong
pearl	진주	jinju
peas	완두콩	wandukong
pedal	페달	pedal
pedestrian crossing	건널목	geonneolmok
pedicure	발톱 손질	baltop sonjil
pen	펜	pen
penalty	벌금	beolgeum
pencil	연필	yeonpil
penis	(남성) 성기	(namseong) seonggi
penknife	주머니 칼	jumeoni kal
people	사람들	saramdeul
pepper, black	후추	huchu
pepper, chilli	고추	gochu
performance	공연	gongyeon
perfume	향수	hyangsu
perhaps, maybe	아마	ama
period (menstrual)	생리	saeng.ni
permit, allow, to	허락하다	heorakhada
person	사람	saram
personal	개인적이다, 개인적인	gaeinjeogida, gaeinjeogin
pet animal	애완동물	aewandongmul
petrol	휘발유	hwiballyu
petrol station	주유소	juyuso
pharmacy, drugstore	약국	yakguk
phone	전화	jeonhwa
phone, to	전화하다	jeonhwahada
phone booth	전화 박스	jeonhwa bakseu
phone card	전화 카드	jeonhwa kadeu

phone directory	전화 번호부	*jeonhwa beonhobu*
phone number	전화 번호	*jeonhwa beonho*
photocopier	복사기	*boksagi*
photocopy	복사	*boksa*
photocopy, to	복사하다	*boksahada*
photograph	사진	*sajin*
photograph, to	사진 찍다	*sajin jjikda*
phrasebook	숙어집	*sugeojip*
pick up (someone), to	태워주다	*taewojuda*
picnic	야유회	*yayuhoe*
pillow	베개	*begae*
pillowcase	베갯잇	*begaennit*
pills, tablets	알약	*allyak*
pin	핀	*pin*
pineapple	파인애플	*painaepeul*
pipe (plumbing)	파이프	*paipeu*
pipe (smoking)	파이프	*paipeu*
pipe tobacco	파이프 담배	*paipeu dambae*
place of interest	관광 명소	*gwan-gwang myeongso*
plain (not flavored)	담백하다/-한	*dambaekhada, dambaekan*
plain (simple)	단순하다, 단순한	*dansunhada, dansunhan*
plan	계획	*gyehoek*
plane	비행기	*bihaenggi*
plant	식물	*singmul*
plastic	플라스틱	*peullaseutik*
plastic bag	비닐 봉지	*binil bongji*
plate	접시	*jeopsi*
platform	플랫포옴	*peullaetpom*
play (drama)	연극	*yeon-geuk*
play (fun), to	놀다	*nolda*
play golf	골프 치다	*golpeu chida*
play sports	운동 경기하다	*undong gyeonggihada*
play tennis	테니스 치다	*teniseu chida*
playground	운동장	*undongjang*
playing cards	카아드 놀이	*kadeu nori*
pleasant	기분 좋다/좋은	*gibun jota/jo-eun*
please (request)	좀 -어/아 주세요	*jom -eo/a juseyo*
pleasure	기쁨	*gippeum*
plug (electric)	플러그	*peulleogeu*
plum	자두	*jadu*
pocket	호주머니	*hojumeoni*
pocketknife	주머니 칼	*jumeoni kal*
point out, to	지적하다	*jijeokhada*
poison	독(약)	*dok(yak)*
poisonous	독이 있다/있는	*dogi itda/inneun*
police	경찰	*gyeongchal*
police officer	경찰관	*gyeongchalgwan*
police station	경찰서	*gyeongchalseo*
pond	연못	*yeonmot*
pony	조랑말	*jorangmal*
population	인구	*in.gu*
pork	돼지고기	*dwaejigogi*
port	항구	*hanggu*

porter (concierge)	수위	*suwi*
porter (for bags)	포터	*poteo*
possible	가능하다, 가능한	*ganeunghada, ganeunghan*
post office	우체국	*ucheguk*
post, mail, to	부치다	*buchida*
postage	우편 요금	*upyeon yogeum*
postage stamp	우표	*upyo*
postbox	우체통	*uchetong*
postcard	엽서	*yeopseo*
post code	우편 번호	*upyeon beonho*
postpone, to	연기하다	*yeon-gihada*
potato	감자	*gamja*
potato chips	감자 튀김	*gamja twigim*
powdered milk	분유	*bunyu*
power outlet	콘센트	*konsenteu*
prawn	새우	*sae-u*
precious metal	귀금속	*gwigeumsok*
precious stone	보석	*boseok*
prefer, to	선호하다	*seonhohada*
preference	선호	*seonho*
pregnant	임신하다, 임신	*imsinhada, imsinhan*
prescription	처방(전)	*cheobang(jeon)*
present (gift)	선물	*seonmul*
present (here)	출석하다, 출석한	*chulseokhada, chulseokan*
press, journalism	언론	*eollon*
pressure	압력	*amnyeok*
price	가격	*gagyeok*
price list	가격표	*gagyeokpyo*
print (photo)	인화	*inhwa*
print, to	인화하다	*inhwahada*
probably	아마	*ama*
problem	문제	*munje*
profession	직업	*jigeop*
profit	이익	*iik*
program, schedule	프로그램	*peurogeuraem*
pronounce, to	발음하다	*bareumhada*
propane	프로판 가스	*peuropan gaseu*
pudding	푸딩	*puding*
pull a muscle	근육 이완	*geunyuk iwan*
pull, to	당기다	*danggida*
pulse	맥박	*maekbak*
pure	순수하다, 순수한	*sunsuhada, sunsuhan*
purify, to	정화하다	*jeonghwahada*
purple	자주색	*jajusaek*
purse (for money)	지갑	*jigap*
push, to	밀다	*milda*
puzzled	어리둥절하다/ -해하다	*eoridungjeolhada/ -haehada*
pyjamas	파자마	*pajama*

Q

quarter	4 분의 1	*sa bunui il*
quarter of an hour	십오분	*sip-obun*
queen	여왕	*yeowang*
question	질문, 문제	*jilmun, munje*

quick	빠르다, 빠른	*ppareuda, ppareun*
quiet	조용하다, 조용한	*joyonghada, joyonghan*

R

radio	라디오	*radio*
railroad, railway	철도	*cheoltto*
rain	비	*bi*
rain, to	비가 오다	*biga oda*
raincoat	비옷	*biot*
rape	강간	*ganggan*
rash	발진	*baljin*
rat	쥐	*jwi*
rate of exchange (for foreign currency)	환율	*hwannyul*
rate, tariff	요금	*yogeum*
raw, uncooked	날 (것의)	*nal (geosui)*
razor blade	면도날	*myeondonal*
read, to	읽다	*iltta*
really (in fact)	실제로	*siljjero*
really?	정말요?	*jeongmaryo?*
reason	이유	*iyu*
receipt	영수증	*yeongsujeung*
receive, to	받다	*batda*
reception desk	안내	*annae*
recipe	조리법	*joribeop*
recommend, to	추천하다	*chucheonhada*
rectangle	직사각형	*jiksagakhyeong*
red	빨갛다, 빨간	*ppalgata, ppalgan*
red wine	적포도주	*jeokpodoju*
reduction	축소	*chukso*
refrigerator	냉장고	*naengjanggo*
refund	환불	*hwanbul*
region	지역, 지방	*jiyeok, jibang*
registered	등록되다, 등록된	*deungnokdoeda, deungnokdoen*
relatives, family	친척	*chincheok*
reliable	믿을 만하다, 믿을 만한	*mideulmanhada, mideulmanhan*
religion	종교	*jonggyo*
remains (historical)	유물	*yumul*
rent out, to	세주다	*sejuda*
rent, to	임대하다	*imdaehada*
repair, to	고치다	*gochida*
repeat, to	반복하다	*banbokhada*
report (police)	보고서	*bogoseo*
reservation	예약	*yeyak*
reserve (ask for in advance), to	예약하다	*yeyakhada*
responsible, to be	책임 있다/있는	*chaegim itda/inneun*
rest, relax, to	쉬다	*swida*
restaurant	식당	*sikdang*
restroom	화장실	*hwajangsil*
result	결과	*gyeolgwa*
retired	퇴직하다, 퇴직한	*toejikhada, toejikan*
return ticket	왕복표	*wangbokpyo*
reverse (car), to	뒤로 가다	*dwiro gada*

Word list

English	Korean	Romanization
rheumatism	류머티즘	ryumeotijeum
ribbon	리본	ribon
rice (cooked)	밥	bap
rice (grain)	쌀	ssal
rice (plant)	벼	byeo
ride, to	타다	tada
ridiculous	어리석다, 어리석은	eoriseokda, eoriseogeun
riding (horseback)	말타기	maltagi
right of way	지금 당장	jigeum dangjang
right, correct	옳다, 옳은	olta, oreun
right-hand side	오른쪽	oreunjjok
rinse	헹굼	henggum
ripe, to	익다, 익은	ikda, igeun
risk	위험	wiheom
river	강	gang
road	도로	doro
roadway	차도	chado
roasted, grilled, toasted	구운	guun
rock (stone)	바위	bawi
roll (bread)	롤빵	rolppang
roof	지붕	jibung
room	방, 룸	bang, rum
room number	룸 넘버	rum neonbeo
room service	룸 서비스	rum seobiseu
rope	밧줄	batjul
route	루트	ruteu
rowing boat	나룻배	narutbae
rubber	고무	gomu
rude	무례하다, 무례한	muryehada, muryehan
ruins	유적	yujeok
run, to	달리다	dallida
running shoes	조깅화	joginghwa

S

sad	슬프다, 슬픈	seulpeuda, seulpeun
safe	안전하다, 안전한	anjeonhada, anjeonhan
safe (for cash)	금고	geumgo
safety pin	안전핀	anjeonpin
sail, to	항해하다	hanghaehada
sailing boat	요트	yoteu
salad	샐러드	saelleodeu
sale (reduced prices)	세일	seil
sales clerk	점원	jeomwon
salt	소금	sogeum
salty	짜다, 짠	jjada, jjan
same	같다, 같은	gatda, gateun
sandals	샌달	saendal
sandy beach	백사장	baeksajang
sanitary towel, sanitary napkin	생리대	saeng.nidae
satisfied	만족하다/ -해하다	manjokhada, manjokaehada
Saturday	토요일	toyoil
sauce	소스, 양념	soseu, yangnyeom

saucepan	냄비	naembi
sauna	사우나	sauna
save, keep, to	보관하다	bogwanhada
say, to	말하다	malhada
scald (injury)	물화상	mulhwasang
scales	저울	jeo.ul
scarf	스카프	seukapeu
scenic walk	전망이 좋은 산책로	jeonmang-i joeun sanchaengno
school	학교	hakgyo
scissors	가위	gawi
Scotland	스코틀랜드	seukoteullaendeu
screw	나사	nasa
screwdriver	드라이버	deuraibeo
scuba diving	스쿠버 다이빙	seukubeo daibing
sculpture	조각	jogak
sea	바다	bada
seafood	해물	haemul
seasick	배멀미	baemeolmi
seat	자리	jari
second (in line)	두 번째	du beonjjae
second (instant), in a	금방	geumbang
second-hand	중고	junggo
sedative	진정제	jinjeongje
see, to	보다	boda
send, to	보내다	bonaeda
sentence	문장	munjang
separate	각각(의)	gakgak(ui)
September	구월	guwol
serious	심각하다, 심각한	simgakhada, simgakan
service	서비스	seobiseu
service station	주유소	juyuso
serviette, table napkin	냅킨	naepkin
sesame oil	참기름	chamgireum
sesame seeds	참깨	chamkkae
set	세트	seteu
sew, to	바느질하다	baneujilhada
shade	그늘	geuneul
shame, disgrace	수치	suchi
shampoo	샴푸	syampu
shark	상어	sang-eo
shave, to	면도하다	myeondohada
shaver	면도기	myeondogi
shaving cream	면도 크림	myeondo keurim
she	그 여자	geu yeoja
her	그 여자의	geu yeoja-ui
sheet (for bed)	시트	siteu
shirt	셔츠	syeocheu
shoe polish	구두약	guduyak
shoes	신발	sinbal
shop assistant	점원	jeomwon
shop window	쇼 윈도우	syowindou
shop, go shopping, to	쇼핑하다	syopinghada
shop, store	가게	gage
shopping center	쇼핑 센터	syoping senteo
short (not tall)	작다, 작은	jakda, jageun

short circuit	합선	*hapseon*
shorts (short trousers)	반바지	*banbaji*
shorts (underpants)	팬티	*paenti*
shoulder	어깨	*eokkae*
show (live performance)	쇼	*syo*
show, to	보여주다	*boyeojuda*
shower, to take a	샤워하다	*syawohada*
shrimp, prawn	새우	*sae-u*
shutter (camera)	셔터	*seoteo*
shutter (on window)	셔터	*seoteo*
sick, ill	아프다, 아픈	*apeuda, apeun*
sieve	체	*che*
sightseeing	시내 관광	*sinae gwan-gwang*
sign (road)	도로 표지	*doro pyoji*
sign, symbol	표시	*pyosi*
sign, to	서명하다	*seomyeonghada*
signature	서명,사인	*seomyeong, ssain*
silent	고요하다, 고요한	*goyohada, goyohan*
silk	실크	*silkeu*
silver	은	*eun*
similar	비슷하다, 비슷한	*biseuthada, biseutan*
simple (easy)	쉽다, 쉬운	*swipda, swiun*
simple (uncomplicated)	간단하다/- 한	*gandanhada, gandanhan*
sing, to	노래하다	*noraehada*
single (only one)	단 하나(의)	*dan hana(ui)*
single (unmarried)	독신(의)	*doksin(ui)*
single ticket	편도표	*pyeondopyo*
sir (term of address)	...님	*...nim*
sister	자매	*jamae*
sit down, to	앉다	*anda*
size	사이즈	*saijeu*
skiing	스키	*seuki*
skin	피부	*pibu*
skirt	치마	*chima*
sleep, to	자다	*jada*
sleeping car	침대칸	*chimdaekan*
sleeping pills	수면제	*sumyeonje*
sleeve	소매	*somae*
slip (petticoat, underskirt)	슬립	*seullip*
slippers	슬리퍼	*seullipeo*
slow	느리다, 느린	*neurida, neurin*
slow train	완행 열차	*wanhaeng yeolcha*
slowly	천천히	*cheoncheonhi*
small	작다, 작은	*jakda, jageun*
small change	잔돈	*jandon*
smell, bad odor	냄새	*naemsae*
smoke	연기	*yeon-gi*
smoke (tobacco), to	담배 피다	*dambae pida*
smoke detector	연기 경보기	*yeon-gi gyeongbogi*
smoked	훈제	*hunje*
snake	뱀	*baem*
sneeze, to	재채기하다	*jaechaegihada*
snore, to	코 골다	*ko golda*
snorkel	스노클링	*seunokeulling*
snow	눈	*nun*
snow, to	눈이 오다	*nuni oda*

soap	비누	*binu*
soap powder	세제	*seje*
soccer	축구	*chukgu*
soccer match	축구 경기	*chukgu gyeonggi*
socket (electric)	소케트	*soketeu*
socks	양말	*yangmal*
soft drink	음료수	*eumnyosu*
sold out	매진	*maejin*
sole (of shoe)	밑창	*mitchang*
somebody, someone	어떤 사람	*eotteon saram*
something	어떤 것	*eotteon geot*
sometimes	가끔	*gakkeum*
somewhere	어딘가	*eodin-ga*
son	아들	*adeul*
soon	곧	*got*
sore throat	인후통	*inhutong*
sore, painful	아프다, 아픈	*apeuda, apeun*
sorry!	미안합니다!	*mianhamnida*
soup (clear)	국	*guk*
soup (spicy stew)	찌개	*jjigae*
sour	시다, 신	*sida, sin*
south	남쪽	*namjjok*
souvenir	기념품	*ginyeompum*
soy sauce	간장	*ganjang*
spanner, wrench	스패너	*seuppaeneo*
spare	스페어	*seuppeeo*
spare parts	부품	*bupum*
spare tyre	스페어 타이어	*seuppeo taieo*
spare wheel	스페어 타이어	*seuppeo taieo*
speak, to	말하다	*malhada*
specialist (doctor)	전문의	*jeonmunui*
speciality (cooking)	특선 요리	*teukseon yori*
speed	속도	*sokdo*
speed limit	제한 속도	*jehan sokdo*
spell, to	철자하다	*cheoljjahada*
spices	양념, 향료	*yangnyeom, hyangnyo*
spicy	맵다, 매운	*maepda, mae.un*
splinter	파편	*papyeon*
spoon	숟가락	*sukkarak*
sports	스포츠	*seupocheu*
sports center	스포츠 센터	*seupocheu senteo*
spot (place)	지점	*jijeom*
spot (stain)	점	*jeom*
spouse	배우자	*bae-uja*
sprain	삠	*ppim*
spray	스프레이	*seupeurei*
spring (device)	용수철	*yongsucheol*
spring (season)	봄	*bom*
square (plaza)	광장	*gwangjang*
square (shape)	정사각형	*jeongsagakhyeong*
square meter	제곱 미터	*jegop miteo*
squash (game)	스쿼시	*seukwosi*
squid	오징어	*ojing-eo*
stadium	스타디움	*seutadium*
staff	직원	*jigwon*

English	Korean	Romanization
stain	얼룩	eolluk
stain remover	얼룩 제거제	eolluk jegeoje
stairs	계단	gyedan
stamp (postage)	우표	upyo
stand up, to	일어서다	ireoseoda
star	별	byeol
start, beginning	시작	sijak
start, to	시작하다	sijakhada
station	역	yeok
stationery	문구	mun-gu
statue	동상	dongsang
stay overnight, to	묵다	mukda
stay, remain, to	머무르다	meomureuda
steal, to	훔치다	humchida
steamed	찌다, 찐	jjida, jjin
steel	강철	gangcheol
stepfather	계부	gyebu
stepmother	계모	gyemo
steps, stairs	계단	gyedan
sterilise, to	소독하다	sodokhada
sticking plaster	반창고	banchanggo
sticky tape	테프	tepeu
stitch (in wound), to	봉합하다	bonghaphada
stomach (abdomen)	배	bae
stomach (organ)	위	wi
stomach ache	복통	boktong
stomach cramps	위 경련	wi gyeongnyeon
stone	돌	dol
stools	대변	daebyeon
stop (bus)	정류장	jeongnyujang
stop, cease	그만두다	geumanduda
stoop, halt to	멈추다	meomchuda
stopover	도중 하차	dojung hacha
store, shop	가게	gage
storey (of a building)	...층 짜리	...cheung jjari
storm	폭풍	pokpung
straight	똑바르다, 똑바른	ttokbareuda, ttokbareun
straight ahead	똑바로	ttokbaro
straw (drinking)	스트로	seuteuro
street	거리	geori
street vendor	자동 판매기	jadong panmaegi
strike (work stoppage)	파업	pa.eop
string	끈	kkeun
strong	힘세다, 힘센	himseda, himsen
student	학생	haksaeng
study (learn), to	공부하다	gongbuhada
stuffed animal	동물 인형	dongmul inhyeong
subtitles	자막	jamak
succeed, to	성공하다	seonggonghada
sugar	설탕	seoltang
suit, business	정장	jeongjang
suitcase	여행가방	yeohaenggabang
summer	여름	yeoreum
sun	태양	taeyang
sunbathe	일광욕	ilgwangyok
Sunday	일요일	iryoil

sunglasses	선글라스	*seon-geullas*
sunlight	햇빛	*haetbit*
sunny	화창하다/-한	*hwachanghada/-han*
sunrise	일출	*ilchul*
sunscreen	썬탠 크림	*seontaen keurim*
sunset	일몰	*ilmol*
sunshade	차일	*chail*
sunstroke	일사병	*ilsabyeong*
suntan lotion	썬탠 로션	*seontaen rosyeon*
suntan oil	썬탠 오일	*seontaen oil*
supermarket	수퍼마켓	*supeomaket*
surcharge	추가 요금	*chuga yogeum*
surf	파도	*pado*
surface mail	선편	*seonyeon*
surfboard	서핑 보드	*seoping bodeu*
surname	성	*seong*
surprised	놀란	*nollan*
swallow, to	삼키다	*samkida*
swamp	습지	*seupji*
sweat	땀	*ttam*
sweat, to	땀 흘리다	*ttam heullida*
sweater	스웨터	*seuweteo*
sweet	달다, 단	*dalda, dan*
sweetcorn	사탕 옥수수	*satang oksusu*
sweets, candy	사탕	*satang*
swim, to	수영하다	*suyeonghada*
swimming costume, swimsuit	수영복	*suyeongbok*
swimming pool	수영장	*suyeongjang*
swindle	사기	*sagi*
switch	스위치	*seuwichi*
syrup	시럽	*sireop*

T

table	테이블	*teibeul*
table tennis	탁구	*takgu*
tablecloth	테이블 보	*teibeul ppo*
table mat	접시 받침	*jeopsi batchim*
tablespoon	테이블 스푼	*teibeul seupun*
tablets	알약	*allyak*
tableware	식탁용구	*siktakyonggu*
take (medicine), to	(약을) 먹다	*(yageul) meokda*
take (photograph), to	(사진을) 찍다	*(sajineul) jjikda*
take (time), to	(시간이) 걸리다	*(sigani) geollida*
take off (clothes), to	벗다	*beotda*
talk, to	말하다	*malhada*
tall	키 크다/큰	*ki keuda/keun*
tampon	탬폰	*taempon*
tap	수도	*sudo*
tap water	수돗물	*sudonmul*
tape measure	줄자	*julja*
tassel	술	*sul*
taste	맛	*mat*
taste, to	맛보다	*matboda*
tasty, delicious	맛있다, 맛있는	*masitda, masinneun*
tax	세금	*segeum*
tax-free shop	면세점	*myeonsejeom*

Word list

taxi	택시	*taeksi*
taxi stand	택시 정류장	*taeksi jeongnyujang*
tea	차	*cha*
tea (green)	녹차	*nokcha*
tea cup	찻잔	*chatjan*
teapot	차 주전자	*cha jujeonja*
teaspoon	티 스푼	*ti seupun*
teat (bottle)	젖병 꼭지	*jeotbyeongkkokji*
teeth	이	*i*
telephoto lens	망원 렌즈	*mang.won lenjeu*
television	텔레비전	*tellebijeon*
telex	텔렉스	*tellekseu*
tell, to	말하다	*malhada*
temperature (body)	체온	*cheon*
temperature (heat)	온도	*ondo*
temple	절	*jeol*
temporary filling	임시 때움	*imsi ttaeum*
tender (sore)	무르다 무른	*mureuda, mureun*
tennis	테니스	*teniseu*
tent	텐트	*tenteu*
terminus	종점	*jongjeom*
terrace	테라스	*teraseu*
terribly	몹시	*mopsi*
test	시험	*siheom*
thank you! thanks!	감사합니다!	*gamsahamnida!*
thaw, to	녹이다	*nogida*
theater (drama)	극장	*geukjang*
theft	도난	*donan*
there	저기에, 거기에	*jeogie, geogie*
thermometer (body)	체온계	*cheongye*
thermometer (weather)	온도계	*ondogye*
they	그들	*geudeul*
thick (of liquids)	진하다, 진한	*jinhada, jinhan*
thick (of things)	두껍다, 두꺼운	*dukkeopda, dukkeo.un*
thief	도둑	*doduk*
thigh	허벅지	*heobeokji*
thin (not fat)	마른	*mareun*
thin (not thick)	묽은	*mulgeun*
thing	물건	*mulgeon*
think, have an opinion, to	생각하다	*saenggakhada*
think, ponder, to	숙고하다	*sukgohada*
third	세 번째	*se beonjjae*
third(1/3), one third	삼분의 일	*sambune il*
thirsty	목마르다, 목마른	*mongmareuda, mongmareun*
this afternoon	오늘 오후	*oneul ohu*
this evening	오늘 저녁	*oneul jeonyeok*
this morning	오늘 아침	*oneul achim*
thread	실	*sil*
throat	목(구멍)	*mok(gumeong)*
throat lozenges	기침 사탕	*gichim satang*
thunderstorm	천둥 폭풍우	*cheondung pokpung-u*
Thursday	목요일	*mogyoil*
ticket	표	*pyo*
ticket office	매표소	*maepyoso*
tidy	단정하다, 단정한	*danjeonghada, danjeonghan*

Word list

15

tie (necktie)	넥타이	nektai
tie, to	매다	maeda
tights, pantyhose	타이즈	taijeu
time (occasion)	시간	sigan
times (multiplying)	...배	...bae
timetable	시간표	siganpyo
tin (can)	깡통	kkangtong
tin opener	깡통 따개	kkangtong ttagae
tip (gratuity)	팁	tip
tissues	티슈	tisyu
tobacco	담배	dambae
today	오늘	oneul
toddler	유아	yua
toe	발가락	balkkarak
together	함께	hamkke
toilet	화장실	hwajangsil
toilet paper	화장지	hwajangji
toilet seat	변기	byeon-gi
toiletries	세면 도구	semyeon dogu
tomato	토마토	tomato
tomorrow	내일	nae-il
tongue	혀	hyeo
tonight	오늘밤	oneulppam
tool, utensil, instrument	도구	dogu
tooth	이	i
toothache	치통	chitong
toothbrush	첫솔	chissol
toothpaste	치약	chiyak
toothpick	이 쑤시개	i ssusigae
top	꼭대기	kkokdaegi
top up, to	채우다	chae-uda
torch, flashlight	손전등	sonjeondeung
total	합계	hapgye
tough	거칠다, 거친	geochilda, geochin
tour	투어	tueo
tour guide	투어 가이드	tueo gaideu
tourist	관광객	gwan-gwanggaek
tourist class	투어 클라스	tueo keullas
tourist information office	관광 안내소	gwan-gwang annaeso
tow, to	끌다	kkeulda
tow cable	케이블	keibeul
towel	수건	sugeon
tower	탑	tap
town	마을, 시	ma-eul, si
town hall	구청	gucheong
toy	장난감	jangnankkam
traffic	교통	gyotong
traffic light	신호등	sinhodeung
train	기차	gicha
train station	역	yeok
train ticket	기차표	gichapyo
train timetable	기차 시간표	gicha siganpyo
translate, to	번역하다	beonyeokhada
travel agent	여행사	yeohaengsa
travel, to	여행하다	yeohaenghada
traveler	여행자	yeohaengja
traveler's cheque	여행자 수표	yeohaengja supyo

Word list

15

tree	나무	*namu*
triangle	삼각형	*samgakhyeong*
trim (haircut), to	(머리를) 다듬다	*(meorireul) dadeumda*
trip, journey	여행	*yeohaeng*
trouble	문제	*munje*
trousers	바지	*baji*
truck	트럭	*teureok*
trust, to	믿다	*mitda*
trustworthy	믿을만한	*mideulmanhan*
try on (clothes), to	입어보다	*ibeo boda*
try on (footwear), to	신어 보다	*sineo boda*
try on (headgear), to	써보다	*sseo boda*
tube (of paste)	튜브	*tyubeu*
Tuesday	화요일	*hwayoil*
tuna	참치	*chamchi*
tunnel	터널	*teoneol*
turn off, to	끄다	*kkeuda*
turn on, to	켜다	*kyeoda*
turn over, to	뒤집다	*dwijipda*
TV	티비	*tibi*
TV guide	티비 방송안내	*tibi bangsong annae*
tweezers	족집게	*jokjipge*
twin-bedded	트윈 베드인	*teuwin bedeuin*
typhoon	태풍	*taepung*
tyre	타이어	*taieo*
tyre pressure	타이어 압력	*taieo amnyeok*

U

ugly	못생기다, 못생긴	*motsaenggida, motsaenggin*
UHT milk	고온 살균 우유	*goon salgyun uyu*
ulcer	궤양	*gweyang*
umbrella	우산	*usan*
under	...아래	*...arae*
underpants	팬티	*paenti*
underpass	지하도	*jihado*
understand, to	이해하다	*ihaehada*
underwear	속옷	*sogot*
undressed, to get	옷 벗다	*ot beotda*
unemployed	실직한	*siljikan*
uneven	고르지 않은	*goreuji aneun*
United States	미국	*miguk*
university	대학	*daehak*
unleaded	무연	*muyeon*
until	...까지, -(으)ㄹ 때까지	*...kkaji, -(eu)l ttaekkaji*
up, upward	...위에, ...위로	*...wie, ...wiro*
upright	똑바른, 똑바로	*ttokbareun, ttokbaro*
urgent	긴급한	*gin-geupan*
urgently	긴급하게	*gin.geupage*
urine	소변	*sobyeon*
use, to	사용하다	*sayonghada*
usually	보통	*botong*

V

vacate, to	비우다	*biuda*
vacation	방학	*banghak*

English	Korean	Romanization
vaccination	예방 접종	yebang jeopjong
vagina	(여성) 성기	(yeoseong) seonggi
valid	유효하다, 유효한	yuhyohada, yuhyohan
valley	계곡	gyegok
valuable	귀중하다, 귀중한	gwijunghada, gwijunghan
valuables	귀중품	gwijungpum
van	봉고차	bonggocha
vase	꽃병	kkotbyeong
vegetables	야채	yachae
vegetarian	채식주의자	chaesikju-uija
vein	정맥	jeongmaek
velvet	벨벳	belbet
vending machine	자동 판매기	jadong panmaegi
venomous	독이 있다, 독이 있는	dogi itda, dogi inneun
venereal disease	성병	seongppyeong
vertical	수직이다, 수직(인)	sujigida, sujig(in)
very	아주	aju
vest, undershirt	조끼	jokki
via	...을/를 거쳐서	...eul/reul geochyeoseo
video camera	비디오 카메라	bidio kamera
video cassette	비디오 (테이프)	bidio (teipeu)
video recorder	비디오 (레코드)	bidio (rekodeu)
view, look at, to	보다	boda
view, panorama	경치	gyeongchi
village	마을	ma-eul
vinegar	식초	sikcho
visa	비자	bija
visit	방문	bangmun
visit, to pay a	방문하다	bangmunhada
visiting time	방문 시간	bangmun sigan
vitamin tablets	비타민(제)	bitamin(je)
vitamins	비타민	bitamin
volcano	화산	hwasan
volleyball	배구	baegu
vomit, to	토 하다	tohada

W

English	Korean	Romanization
wait for, to	기다리다	gidarida
waiter	종업원	jong.eobwon
waiting room	대기실	daegisil
waitress	종업원	jong-eobwon
wake someone up, to	깨우다	kkae-uda
wake up, to	깨어나다	kkae-eonada
walk (noun)	걷기	geotgi
walk, to	걷다	geotda
walking stick	지팡이	jipang-i
wall	벽	byeok
wallet	지갑	jigap
want, to	...을/를 원하다, -고 싶다	...eul/reul wonhada, -go sipda
wardrobe	옷장	otjang
warn, to	경고하다	gyeonggohada
warning	경고	gyeonggo
wash, to	씻다	ssitda

washing	세탁	*setak*
washing line	빨랫줄	*ppallaetjul*
washing machine	세탁기	*setakgi*
wasp	벌	*beol*
watch (wristwatch)	(손목)시계	*(sonmok)sigye*
watch, look, see, to	보다	*boda*
water	물	*mul*
water-skiing	수상 스키	*susang seuki*
waterfall	폭포	*pokpo*
watermelon	수박	*subak*
waterproof	방수	*bangsu*
way (direction)	쪽	*jjok*
way (method)	방법	*bangbeop*
way in	입구	*ipgu*
way out	출구	*chulgu*
we, us	우리	*uri*
weak	약하다, 약한	*yakhada, yakan*
wear, to	입다	*ipda*
weather	날씨	*nalssi*
weather forecast	일기예보	*ilgiyebo*
wedding	결혼식	*gyeolhonsik*
Wednesday	수요일	*suyoil*
week	주	*ju*
weekday	주중	*jujung*
weekend	주말	*jumal*
weigh, to	...의 무게를 달다	*...ui mugereul dalda*
weigh out, to	달아내다	*daranaeda*
welcome!	어서 오세요!	*eoseo oseyo!*
well (for water)	우물	*umul*
well (good)	잘	*jal*
west	서쪽	*seojjok*
westerner	서양 사람	*seoyang saram*
wet	젖다, 젖은	*jeotda, jeojeun*
wetsuit	_수트	*wetsuteu*
what?	뭐라고요?	*mworagoyo?*
wheel	바퀴	*bakwi*
wheelchair	휠체어	*hwilcheeo*
when?	언제요?	*eonjeyo?*
whenever	-(으)ㄹ 때마다	*-(eu)l ttaemada*
where to?	어디로 가세요?	*eodiro gaseyo?*
where?	어디요?	*eodiyo?*
which?	어느 거요?	*eoneu geoyo?*
white	하얗다, 하얀	*hayata, hayan*
white wine	백포도주	*baekpodoju*
who?	누구요?	*nuguyo?*
why?	왜요?	*waeyo?*
widow	과부	*gwabu*
widower	홀아비	*horabi*
wife	아내	*anae*
wind, breeze	바람	*baram*
window (for paying, buying tickets)	창구	*changgu*
window (in house)	창문	*changmun*
windscreen wiper	와이퍼	*waipeo*
windscreen, windshield	(자동차) 앞유리	*(jadongcha) amnyuri*
wine	포도주	*podoju*
winter	겨울	*gyeo-ul*

wire	철사	*cheolssa*
wish, to	바라다	*barada*
witness	목격자	*mokgyeokja*
woman	여자	*yeoja*
wonderful	멋지다, 멋진	*meotjida, meotjin*
wood	나무	*namu*
wool	울, 양모	*ul, yangmo*
word	단어	*daneo*
work, occupation	일, 직업	*il, jigeop*
work, to	일하다	*ilhada*
working day	근무일	*geunmuil*
worn out (clothes)	닳아버리다/-버린	*darabeorida, darabeorin*
worn out, tired	피곤하다, 피곤한	*pigonhada, pigonhan*
worry, to	걱정하다	*geokjeonghada*
wound	상처	*sangcheo*
wrap, to	싸다	*ssada*
wrench, spanner	스패너	*seupaeneo*
wrist	손목	*sonmok*
write down	적다	*jeokda*
write, to	쓰다	*sseuda*
writing pad	공책	*gongchaek*
writing paper	편지지	*pyeonjiji*
wrong (mistaken)	틀리다, 틀린	*teullida, teullin*

Y

yawn	하품	*hapum*
year	년	*nyeon*
years old	...살, ...세	*...sal, ...se*
yellow	노랗다, 노란	*norata, noran*
yes	네, 예	*ne, ye*
yes please	네, 그렇게 해 주세요.	*ne, geureoke hae juseyo*
yesterday	어제	*eoje*
you (audience)	여러분	*yeoreobun*
you (familiar)	너, 너희(들)	*neo, neohui(deul)*
you (female)	아가씨, 아주머니	*agassi, ajumeoni*
you (male)	아저씨, 선생님	*ajeossi, seonsaengnim*
you're welcome (to thanks)	괜찮아요!	*gwaenchanayo!*
youth hostel	유스 호스텔	*yuseu hoseutel*

Z

zip (fastener)	지퍼	*jipeo*
zoo	동물원	*dongmurwon*
zucchini	애호박	*aehobak*

Word list

15

Basic grammar

1 Word order

Unlike in English, the Korean verb (action verb or adjectival verb) comes at the end of a sentence or clause. Also the Korean word order is quite flexible because there are special markers attached to the words in a sentence. They are called particles, and they mark the function of the words in a sentence: which word is a subject or an object etc. By contrast, in English you cannot simply change the word order in a sentence without violating its meaning because the position of words in a sentence tells us which is a subject or an object. For example, two different sentences, 'The cat chased a mouse' and 'A mouse chased the cat' have the same meaning in Korean because of the particles affixed to the subject and the object respectively: 'The cat-*ga* a mouse-*reul* chased' and 'A mouse-*reul* the cat-*ga* chased' (*ga* indicates 'the cat' is a subject, *reul* indicates 'a mouse' is an object).

2 Common participle

Some of the common particles are:

Subject marker: *i* (이) (after a word ending in a consonant), *ga* (가) (after a word ending in a vowel);

Topic/contrast marker: *eun* (은) (after a word ending in a consonant), *neun* (는) (after a word ending in a vowel);

Object marker: *eul* (을) (after a word ending in a consonant), *reul* (를) (after a word ending in a vowel);

Place/time marker (in/at/on) : *e* (에) (a place marker *eseo* (에서) has a special usage but it is not covered here)

3 Subject omission

Although the subject comes at the beginning of the sentence, it is often omitted if it is clearly understood from the context by the participants in a conversation.

Where do you live?	*eodi saseyo?*	(where live?)
I live in Sydney	*sidenie sarayo*	(Sydney live)
What are you doing?	*mwo haeyo?*	(what do?)
I am studying	*gongbuhaeyo*	(study)

4 Action verb and adjectival verb

Korean adjectives conjugate like verbs, therefore they are often called adjectival verbs or descriptive verbs. To distinguish a normal verb from an adjectival verb or a descriptive verb, a normal verb is called an action verb. You can see most of the adjectives in the glossary section of this book have two entries, one in a dictionary form which ends in -*da* (다) and the other in an adjectival form which modifies a noun in front of it. Verb conjugation is carried out by adding infixes or suffixes to the verb stem. The verb stem is the part of the verb remaining after -*da* (다) is taken away from the dictionary form of the verb.

5 Honorific language

When you speak Korean, you have to know who you are talking to. Depending on your relationship with them, their age and their social status, you have to choose an appropriate level of politeness when you talk. There are several speech levels in Korean. These speech levels are indicated in a sentence by the sentence-final suffixes attached to the end of verb stems. We will not cover all these levels here. We will only talk about the most common polite endings, which travelers are most likely to use in a real situation: formal polite form, informal polite form and informal honorific form.

Formal polite form
This is used in formal situations, and is common in men's conversation. You add -*mnida* (ㅂ니다) if the verb stem ends in a vowel. Otherwise, you add -*seumnida* (습니다). If you want to make a question sentence, you simply change the final -*da* (다) of these formal polite verb-endings into *kka?* (까?).

Informal polite form
This is common in daily conversation, and is especially used by women. This form requires a bit more complicated process compared to the others. Firstly you have to look at the final vowel of the verb stem. If it is *a* (아) or *o* (오), you add -*ayo* (아요). Otherwise you add -*eoyo* (어요). If the verb stem ends in a vowel, you come to have two consecutive vowels after this conjugation. Two consecutive vowels are usually required to be fused into one. For example, *o* (오) and *a* (아) become *wa* (와). If the two consecutive vowels are the same vowel, one of them will be eliminated. If the verb stem ends in *eu* (으), which is the weakest vowel in Korean, it will also be eliminated.

There are a couple of exceptions to this conjugation rule. If the verb stem ends in *ha* (하), you always change this *ha* (하) into *haeyo* (해요). For the verb *ida* (이다) (to be: equation), you change this particular verb into *yeyo* (예요) after a word ending in a vowel. Otherwise you change this into *ieyo* (이에요). To make a question sentence, you simply say the same sentence with a rising tone at the end as you normally do in a question. There is no grammatical change between a statement and a question sentence in this level of language.

Informal honorific form
When you talk to the people clearly superior to you, such as your clients or guests, much older people or socially high-ranking people, you use an honorific form of language to show your respect to them. Of course you never use this form to refer to yourself. The process of this conjugation is quite simple. You add -*seyo* (세요) if the verb stem ends in a vowel. Otherwise, you add -*euseyo* (으세요).

Too many levels to work out which one to use? Don't panic! They are all polite forms at least. Whichever form you use, you are still in the range of common expectation from the native Korean speakers. Anyway, they often use a mixture of all these levels of language even in a conversation with the same person.

6 Some useful grammatical items

The following grammatical items might help you to make new sentences as long as you know the words.

Would/Could you do something for me?

(*jom*) verb stem + *a/eo jusigesseoyo?*

(좀) verb stem + 아/어 주시겠어요?

If the final vowel in the verb stem is *a* (아) or *o* (오), you choose -*a* (아). Otherwise you choose -*eo* (어). Please refer to the section on 'informal polite form' for more details on how to add -*a/eo* (-아/어), how to deal with consecutive vowels and the exception of *ha* (하) etc.

to fix, 고치다, gochida	...*jom gochyeo jusigesseoyo?*	Could you fix ...?
to find, 찾다, chatda	...*jom chaja jusigesseoyo?*	Could you find ...?
to see, 보다, boda	...*jom bwa jusigesseoyo?*	Could you see ...?

Please do something (for me)

(*jom*) verb stem + *a/eo juseyo?*

(좀) verb stem + 아/어 주세요?

Please refer to the above to see how you add -*a* (아) or -*o* (오).

to fix, 고치다, gochida	...*jom gochyeo juseyo?*	Please fix ...
to write down, 쓰다, sseuda	...*jom sseo juseyo?*	Please write ...down
to see, 보다, boda	...*jom bwa juseyo?*	Please see ...

Don't do it, please

verb stem + *ji maseyo*

verb stem + 지 마세요

to eat, 먹다, meokda	...*meokji maseyo*	Don't eat ..., please
to smoke, 담배 피우다, dambae piuda	*dambae piuji maseyo*	Don't smoke, please
to come, 오다, oda	*oji maseyo*	Don't come, please

I want to do something

verb stem + *go sipeoyo*

verb stem + 고 싶어요

to go, 가다, gada	*gago sipeoyo*	I want to go
to see, 보다, boda	...-*reul/eul bogo sipeoyo*	I want to see ...
to buy, 사다, sada	...-*reul/eul sago sipeoyo*	I want to buy ...